Write about It!

Write about It!

Tools for Developing Writers

Melinda Roth Sayavedra and Joyce Bryan

Ann Arbor

THE UNIVERSITY OF MICHIGAN PRESS

Acknowledgments

We would like to give special thanks to Jerry Bryan and Rusty Van Rossmann for their artwork and to Luis Sayavedra Soto for the photos. Thanks also to the participants of the Writers' Workshop for field testing the material and to the students of the English Language Institute at Oregon State University who worked with the material. Finally, we would like to express our deep appreciation to Leslie Bishop, who offered some very valuable suggestions, and to Dr. Deborah Healey for her skillful guidance in the use of electronic conferencing options.

Preface

Write about It! guides students in discovering the writing processes that work best for them. It can serve as either a companion text to *Talk about It!* or a core text for a writing course. Both are theme-based, interactive texts designed for ESL students at the low-intermediate level in intensive English programs at universities, in community colleges, and in high schools. *Talk about It!* emphasizes speaking, listening, and reading skills while *Write about It!* emphasizes writing skills. Using the two together provides teachers with a complete, integrated program for their low-intermediate ESL students.

One of the guiding principles behind this book is the idea that good writing comes from a process of trial and error, write and rewrite. We realize that there is a very fine line between fostering the process and offering activities that are too controlling. One of the ways we work through this dilemma is by engaging the new writer in topics that elicit strong feelings and activities that lead to meaningful communication. The deliberately bold topics force students to think critically about timely issues and their own reactions to them. They challenge students to reach beyond their current language level, to make their own connections, and to express their own ideas, thus ensuring the emergence of their own unique voices. Students are given opportunities to write on both a personal level and a more formal, expository level.

The text starts with topics that students have knowledge about and experience with so that the beginning writer can jump right into prewriting activities without a great deal of preliminary research. Later units introduce beginning research skills where students are asked to locate outside sources and synthesize the information they find. The emphasis here is on learning the process of research, rather than producing a perfectly finished product.

The prewriting activities in each unit help students focus on the topic, develop vocabulary, form connections with their own knowledge and experiences, and develop strategies to organize their thoughts before writing. We include brainstorming and discussion activities, information-gathering activities, freewrite exercises, samples of authentic writing from student writers, and more. Students are introduced to various organizing strategies and guidelines for starting a paper and for revising drafts. Because writing is not an exact science, we encourage teachers to discuss with students various possibilities in analyzing the samples and in doing the exercises.

In several units in *Write about It!* we have suggested the use of films, videos, audiocassette recordings, and recorded excerpts from radio and TV for the classroom. They bring variety and authenticity to the classroom. However, before presenting a film, video, audiocassette recording, TV or radio excerpt, teachers should check with their institutions to find out the established policies for using copyrighted material of this kind. While policies may vary from institution to institution, it seems reasonably clear among copyright specialists that there is a distinction made between "public" use and "educational" or "instructional" use. Instructional use generally means that the material is not being used for entertainment purposes or for cultural improvement, only for educational purposes. Obviously, copies of the materials cannot be made and distributed to the students. Teachers should check with their institutions to verify that there is no policy against using copyrighted films, videos, audiocassette recordings, and recorded excerpts from radio and TV in their classrooms for educational purposes and what the parameters of "educational use" are.

Contents

To the Teacher

Write about It! offers some unique features to low-intermediate ESL students and their teachers including

- self-evaluations for students
- peer feedback activities
- teacher feedback forms
- ideas for electronic conferencing
- ideas for journal assignments
- ideas for extending the lesson
- guidelines and checklists for revising and polishing papers
- activities to prepare students to complete a short research paper

Each unit of *Write about It!* is designed around a different topic. The pre- and post-writing activities vary from unit to unit but include the following types of exercises.

Get the Picture

Get the Picture activities are used as warm-ups to the various writing tasks. Pictures and questions stimulate vocabulary and ideas about the theme of the unit.

Get Set

Students are asked to work together to brainstorm about the topic—gaining vocabulary, ideas, and insight about the topic from their classmates. This brainstorming session prepares students for freewriting.

Freewrite

In freewrite exercises, students are encouraged to express their thoughts and ideas without regard to form, to simply write, without stopping, for a period of 10 minutes. The freewrite exercises allow students to connect the topics with their own experiences

and knowledge. This activity also gives students the opportunity to use recently ac-
quired vocabulary to express their thoughts and ideas. It is through freewriting that
students discover just how much they already know about a topic, often to their surprise and delight.

Go for It

The readings in this book are purposefully woven in as necessary components of the
writing process. As readers, we are stimulated by the words and ideas of others. We
feel moved to respond to, to question, to rebut or to embrace the ideas of others
through writing. Students learn that writing demands reflection and is often the
catalyst for action. They learn that reading and writing are not separate skills but
are in fact related in a natural codependence.

Work It Out

In Work It Out activities, students are asked to analyze readings—how they are organized, whether they are cohesive, who they were written for, what a writer can learn
from them, and so on. These are opportunities for teachers and students to share
what they think makes a piece of writing effective.

Give-and-Take   # Get Ready

Get Going   # Get Real

The other activities in the book support those exercises that precede or follow them.
They are designed to help beginning writers develop both reading and writing strategies and give students more opportunities to practice important skills.

Pull It Together

In Pull It Together students get a look back at what they have already done in the unit
and are assigned the culminating writing task. We suggest that students be asked to
keep these completed writing assignments in a binder. Teachers may want students to

revise one or more of the papers at a time when students have gained additional skills and confidence, or teachers may want to look back at previous assignments with students during one-on-one conferences to help students see how their writing has developed over time.

Just Do It

All of the units in *Write about It!* include a peer review activity. Peer review activities provide more feedback for writers to think about. Peers are not asked to judge their classmates' papers but to act as another pair of eyes for the writer. They are asked to describe and sometimes to react to what they read. The benefits of peer feedback are threefold: (1) each writer becomes aware of what at least one other reader sees in the paper; (2) the reader/writer is exposed to different voices writing on similar topics; (3) the teacher gains a helper in the feedback process for each writer.

Evaluate Yourself

After each peer feedback activity, students are asked to evaluate their own papers, look back at them with a critical eye, and take ownership of them. These self-evaluations are intended to help students see writing as a personal and interactive process between the writer and the words. There is room on the forms for students to let their teacher know where they are having trouble in their writing so that the teacher can help students where students feel they need it most at that time.

Teacher Feedback

You may or may not choose to use the Teacher Feedback forms. They are included to remind the teacher to look at both the structure and the content of student papers. The feedback form is merely a guide to the teacher, and teachers should feel free to add whatever they feel is important for students to be focusing on in their writing and omit whatever seems unnecessary for their particular students. Each Teacher Feedback form ends with a space for the teacher to focus on what was interesting and successful in the paper. The pages in *Write about It!* (as in *Talk about It!*) are perforated so students can tear out assignments and evaluations to hand in.

Polish It

The Appendix of *Write about It!* is a checklist for writers to use during final editing of their papers. We suggest that students be introduced to the checklist at the end of Unit 3 and that they continue to refer to it in subsequent units. You may want students to focus only on certain items on the checklist, adding more as their writing develops, or you may want them to check through each item for every paper. You may choose to individualize for each student depending on his/her skill level.

Every student's writing conveys a unique voice, and every student's writing is distinct in its weaknesses. *Write about It!* does not focus on teaching grammar because grammatical weaknesses are different for every writer. We encourage teachers to supply grammar instruction to individuals or groups of students based on actual errors occurring in students' papers. At this stage, we feel it is important to focus most attention on the writer's successes in communicating ideas and feelings.

Live and Learn

Additional Activities and Journal Assignments

Each unit ends with ideas for additional activities and journal assignments. We offer them to add variety and additional practice. Teachers should read through the list during the planning stages of preparing to teach the unit. Many of them are appropriate to use at the beginning or middle of the unit as well as at the end.

Journals

We suggest that teachers have students keep a journal for informal writing assignments. Ideas for journal assignments are listed in the Live and Learn section at the end of each unit.

Teachers may want to alternate regular journal assignments with double-entry journal responses. In double-entry journal responses classmates read passages from each other's journals and respond to specific sentences or ideas. The format for double-entry journals is a divided page with the chosen passages and sentences on one side and the classmate's response on the opposite side. We have found that students spend more time on journals when they know that their peers are going to read and respond to their ideas. Interactive journal writing creates a community of writers who can take risks and feel supported.

Connecting to the Real World (1)

We encourage teachers to create a real audience to read students' work. In order to do this, teachers may want to contact a high school or college teacher of native speakers who might be interested in receiving a booklet on cultural differences, personal narratives coming from international writers, exposés on health issues, or any of the other topics included in *Write about It!* Teachers may want to do an exchange of papers between the students and their real audience several times throughout the course and, perhaps, meet for a get-together at the end of the course.

Connecting to the Real World (2)

Teachers have long considered face-to-face conferencing with students a part of their regular teaching assignment. With the current exploding advances in technology, conferencing online is fast becoming common practice for teachers as well. As with anything, there are positives and negatives to online conferencing, but the reality is that we live in an increasingly electronic world that will only continue to command the attention of our students. On the positive side, it is exciting to see students participate in authentic written communication with all of their classmates. Many of our students already feel comfortable with electronic means of communication. For them it is similar to sending their daily e-mail messages.

There are many different types of online conferencing that "can be individual or group, real-time ('synchronous'—as I type, you read what I'm saying and can reply immediately) or delayed ('asynchronous,' like e-mail where I write now and you read and reply later). It can be as cheap as a free site on the Web or e-mail or in the form of a high-priced network package" (Healey 1998).

There are many conferencing sites commercially available, and quite a few free sites have become popular. The site we used in our field testing is a free site called Nicenet: (http://www.nicenet.net). It is intended as an electronic classroom assistant. This site offers conferencing capabilities that provide a forum for all students to interact with each other in writing. It offers conferencing, e-mail, and web linking. The possibilities for its use are many.

- Teachers can create and control the topics to which students respond, or students can generate their own topics.
- Teachers can post the first message; students can reply to it or to the messages of other students.
- Students can edit or delete their own messages.

- Students and teachers can send e-mail to each other and reply privately to some-one who has posted a message.
- Teachers can add links to other websites.
- Teachers can post their schedules, note time changes, and announce special events.
- Teachers can put documents for which they have received copyright permission online for students to see and use. (Teachers should check with their institution to find out the established policies for using copyrighted material.)

Traditionally, feedback has meant the teacher responding to each student's finished work, teacher as corrector. Web-based conferencing allows the teacher to become a collaborator and coach rather than a corrector. It fosters the sharing of ideas through writing. It provides an additional connection to the students' own experiences and validates their words and ideas. We have included tips for using electronic conferencing in the Live and Learn section of each unit.

REFERENCE
Healey, D. 1998. Tech Tips, http://osu.orst.edu/dept/eli/sept1998.html [1998, September].

Unit 1   Getting the Hang of It

Writing about Personal Experiences: Paragraphs about Cultural Differences

Getting the hang of it means _____

Get the Picture

Is the man in this picture being rude?

Why is this little girl smiling?

Has this man made a mistake?

Would this be acceptable in
your country?

In your country, when is it
okay for men to touch?

Give-and-Take

Interview three of your classmates. Ask them to give you a specific example of a cultural difference between their country and North America. Write their observations in the chart.

In North America	In My Classmate's Country
Person #1	Person #1
Person #2	Person #2
Person #3	Person #3

Get Set

Use the following cluster diagram to brainstorm ideas about cultural differences. What are some cultural differences you have noticed between your culture and this culture?

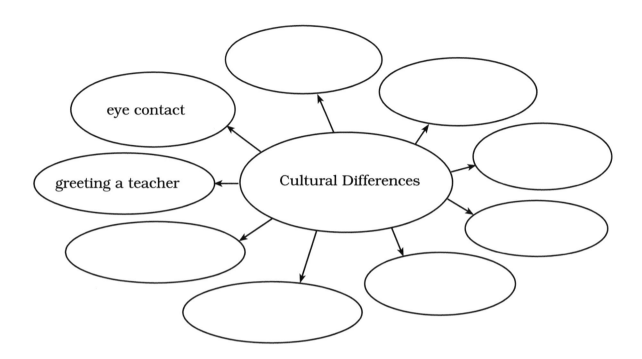

eye contact

greeting a teacher

Cultural Differences

Discuss your ideas with your classmates and add any new ideas to your cluster diagram.

Freewrite

Choose one of the cultural differences you and your classmates have come up with and spend 10 minutes writing about it on a separate sheet of paper. Try to write without stopping. Doing a freewrite exercise helps writers formulate ideas. It is a useful tool when you find you are having trouble getting your ideas down on paper. Keep this freewrite exercise for later use.

Get Ready: Part 1

A. This unit contains a number of paragraphs written by students to express the cultural differences that they observed after arriving in a new culture. As you read the sample paragraph that follows, decide whether one of the sentences tells the reader what the paragraph is about.

This sentence is called the **topic sentence.** It is often the first sentence of a paragraph; however, it can be located anywhere in the paragraph. After you have decided which sentence in the sample paragraph is the topic sentence, write it in the space provided.

Sample Paragraph	*Topic Sentence and Supporting Ideas*
Oriental house customs, especially in Korea and Japan, are very different from Western house customs. In oriental cultures, people do not enter their houses with their shoes on. In Western culture, people wear their shoes inside their houses as a matter of course. In Korea and Japan, the heating system in ancient times was feeding a fire with firewood and the heat traveled through the floor. The present heat delivery system is the same as during ancient times except that instead of using firewood, they now use coal, oil, gas, or electricity. People have not worn their shoes in the house for hundreds of years, so it is very difficult to change this custom.	**Topic Sentence:** **Support:** Examples: People from oriental cultures remove shoes before entering a house; westerners traditionally do not. Explanations: It is difficult to change the custom of removing shoes because people have done this for hundreds of years. Details: Instead of using firewood, they use coal, oil, gas, or electricity. Fact: In ancient Korea and Japan, fires kept the floors warm.

B. The other sentences in the paragraph are called **supporting sentences.** They support and develop the main idea of the paragraph as stated in the topic sentence by giving

　　1.   more details (extra descriptive information),
　　2.   definitions of terms,
　　3.   explanations or reasons,

4. examples,

5. statistics or facts that one might find in a reference book about the topic,

6. other support such as an expert viewpoint, the pros and cons, a personal observation or experience, and so on.

The supporting ideas for the sample paragraph have been identified for you. Discuss them with your class.

C. The last, or concluding, sentence of a paragraph also supports the topic sentence and often closes the paragraph by summing up the main idea discussed in the paragraph.

Does the concluding sentence in this paragraph support the topic sentence?
__ yes   __ no

Discuss this with your class.

Get Ready: Part 2

Work alone or with a partner to complete the following exercise.

A. First, identify the topic sentences in the next three paragraphs and write them in the boxes.

B. Read the supporting sentences in each paragraph and identify the kinds of support they give: examples, explanations, details, facts, and so on. Write the kinds of support in the boxes. Refer back to the sample paragraph for help.

C. Do all of the sentences in the paragraph relate directly to the topic sentence, or do some of them stray from the topic? Circle any sentences that don't directly relate to the topic.

D. Read the concluding sentence for each of the three paragraphs and decide whether it supports the topic sentence. Check yes or no in the space provided.

E. Could paragraph 1 be divided into more than one paragraph? Discuss this with your class.

Paragraph 1	*Topic Sentence and Supporting Ideas*
In different countries we can find so many cultural differences; they can be the way of speaking, the body language, or the way people act and react. These differences are sometimes difficult for a newcomer because some of the things newcomers do might be considered impolite or rude. One difference between my country, Indonesia, and the United States is in how people hand things to each other. In Indonesia people always hand something to someone using their right hand. If they use their left hand, it is considered impolite and not respectful. I remember once I was using public transportation in my country and I was carrying a heavy bag in my right hand. So, I took my money from my left pocket with my left hand and gave it to the driver with my left hand. The driver was angry with me and warned me not to do this again, so I apologized to him. This might sound strange, but these differences are also interesting.	Topic Sentence: Support: The concluding sentence supports the topic sentence. __ yes __ no

Paragraph 2	Topic Sentence and Supporting Ideas
I am a Muslim woman from Afghanistan. Both my religion and my culture teach me to be modest in dress. I wear a burqa, a robe and scarf, to cover myself. Many Americans view my covering up from head to toe as a sort of prison for me. But quite the opposite is true. For me it is a great freedom. I am taken more seriously. People do not form opinions about me based on my looks. They must get to know me through my words and deeds. My brain is valued above my looks. I feel more respected, not less, especially by men. Men in my culture don't have to cover up. I have a hard time understanding how American women can tolerate the disrespect that often comes with immodest dress.	Topic Sentence: Support: The concluding sentence supports the topic sentence. __ yes __ no

Paragraph 3	Topic Sentence and Supporting Ideas
In a Chinese family the elders are very important family members. Old people are not treated well in every culture, but in the traditional Chinese family, elders are treated with respect. We must take good care of our grandparents and parents. They have given us life and all the things we need during our childhood. They are the link to our ancestors. Children have many privileges when they are very young. Our job, as chil-	Topic Sentence: Support:

dren, is to study hard and learn so that when we are older, we can take care of our parents in their old age. We would never think of putting them in a nursing home to spend their last days alone. It is a great honor to make our parents' last years comfortable in the family home.

The concluding sentence supports the topic sentence. __ yes __ no

Get Going

The following paragraphs do *not* have topic sentences. Read the supporting sentences and then write a topic sentence for each paragraph. Remember that the topic sentence doesn't have to be the first sentence in the paragraph. You decide where the topic sentence should go. When you have finished, share your ideas with the class.

Paragraph A

North Americans seem to smile only when they are happy or pleased. For the Vietnamese, a smile is a way of expressing and hiding many different emotions. Vietnamese people will smile to make others feel comfortable, to please them, or to avoid hurting them. Even if they are not interested or disagree with something, Vietnamese people will smile. They will smile when they are embarrassed or disappointed. They will smile if they disagree or if they feel shame. They will also smile when they are happy or pleased. They will smile when they agree and when they feel proud. It is usually hard for non-Vietnamese to understand the real meaning behind a Vietnamese smile. Among the Vietnamese we come to understand the meaning of a smile depending on the situation. The smile gives us a clue that a person is feeling a strong emotion, and then we figure out what that emotion is.

Your topic sentence: _____

_____

Position in the paragraph: _____

What kind of supporting sentences does this paragraph have? (Example: explanation, details)

Does the concluding sentence support the topic sentence of the paragraph?
__ yes   __ no

Paragraph B

A Thai may lend a close friend money and only let that friend know through another friend that he or she needs that money back. A Thai would never scold a friend for getting drunk. While he was drunk, his friends would handle the situation. And Thais do not tell their personal problems and frustrations to their friends. Deep emotions are usually kept to oneself or perhaps shared with an elder brother or sister, a parent, a teacher, or a monk.

Your topic sentence: _____

_____

Position in the paragraph: _____
What kind of supporting sentences does this paragraph have? (Example: explanation)

Does the concluding sentence support the topic sentence of the paragraph?
__ yes   __ no

Paragraph C

Most Mexican people will never understand how Americans can spend so much time and money taking care of their pets. How is it that Americans become so emotionally attached to animals? Pets become like members of the family, but they are only animals. Some Americans seem to take closer care of their pets than they do of their children. They take them to the park daily. They take them to the veterinarian yearly. Some Americans even brush their dogs' teeth!

Your topic sentence: _____

_____

Position in the paragraph: _____

What kind of supporting sentences does this paragraph have? (Example: explanation)

Does the concluding sentence support the topic sentence of the paragraph?

__ yes   __ no

Get Real

A.   The following cluster diagram shows three topic sentences. With some classmates, discuss what kind of information might support these topic sentences. As you and your classmates discuss each one, write down some supporting ideas in the bubbles provided. Feel free to add more bubbles if you need them.

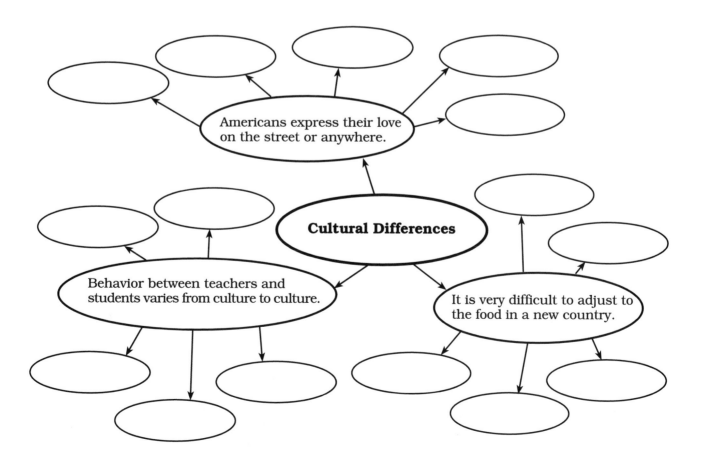

B. Now, on your own, choose one of these topic sentences and write a complete paragraph about it on a separate piece of paper. Remember that each supporting sentence should relate directly to the topic sentence and that the concluding sentence should support the topic sentence and sum up the main idea of the paragraph. Hand your paragraph in to your teacher.

Pull It Together

So far in this unit,

- you have gathered information about cultural differences;
- you have done a freewrite exercise on the topic of cultural differences;
- you have read and analyzed paragraphs about cultural differences;
- you have developed a complete paragraph from a topic sentence.

Now write a paragraph about one of the cultural differences you have explored in class or identify and write about a completely new cultural difference.

You may want to use the freewrite exercise you completed earlier to help you get started.

Your class might consider putting together a booklet for native speakers who may be unfamiliar with your culture. Write with this audience in mind.

First, write your topic sentence in the space provided and then brainstorm supporting ideas to help you develop your main point.

My topic sentence is _____

_____

Possible Supporting Ideas

Now you are ready to write your paragraph. This will be your first draft. When you are finished, exchange your paragraph with a classmate. Read your classmate's paragraph and answer the questions in Just Do It.

Just Do It

Exchange books with a classmate. Then answer the following questions about your classmate's paragraph.

1. Write the topic sentence of the paragraph here.

2. Do the supporting sentences support the topic sentence by giving (circle as many as are appropriate)

    a. details?   c. statistics/facts?   e. definitions?
    b. examples?   d. explanations?   f. other? (identify)

3. Do all of the sentences relate directly to the topic sentence, or do some of them stray from the topic? Write any sentences that don't directly relate to the topic sentence here.

4. Write the concluding sentence of your classmate's paragraph here. Compare it with the topic sentence that you wrote in #1. Does the concluding sentence support and/or sum up the topic sentence of the paragraph?

After answering the questions, return your classmate's book and the paragraph to your classmate. Read your classmate's responses to your paragraph and revise your first draft by making any changes that you want to make to it.

Evaluate Yourself   Name _____

Read your revised paragraph about cultural differences and fill in the following form.

1. My topic sentence is

2. Every sentence in my paragraph relates directly to my topic.
    __ yes   __ no

3. My conclusion supports the topic sentence of my paragraph.
    __ yes   __ no

4. I'm having trouble with

After you have completed this form, decide whether your paragraph needs further revision. Make any changes you wish to make to your paragraph. Now give your original paragraph, your revisions, your final paragraph, and this self-evaluation to your teacher.

Teacher Feedback

Student's Name _____

Structure

1. The topic sentence is

2. Check one.

   __ a. All of your supporting sentences relate directly to your topic sentence.
   __ b. Most of your supporting sentences relate directly to your topic sentence; however, the following sentence seems to be off the topic.
   __ c. Some of your supporting sentences relate directly to your topic sentence; however, the following sentences seem to be off the topic.

3. Your conclusion supports your topic sentence.
   __ yes   __ no
4. One grammar structure that you seem to be having difficulty with is

Content

1. What I find most interesting about your paragraph is

2. What I'd like to know more about is

3. Other comments

Live and Learn

Additional Activities and Journal Assignments

1. Work with your teacher and classmates to compile your paragraphs into a booklet about cultural differences. Share your booklet with some native English speakers. (Teachers, read Connecting to the Real World (1) in the To the Teacher section of this book for ideas on sharing papers with native speakers.)

2. Brainstorm a list of gestures that are common to your culture and your class-mates' cultures. Demonstrate and discuss them in class. Ask your teacher to demonstrate common gestures used here that may differ from the ones you've discussed. Talk about appropriate and inappropriate gestures. Choose one gesture to write about in your journal.

3. Write a letter to a friend in your country explaining some of the cultural differences you have discovered here. You may want to share this letter with a tutor or friend who is a native speaker of English.

4. Write in your journal about a language or cultural misunderstanding that you have experienced here.

5. In your journal, describe what you have learned about writing while doing this unit.

6. Online Conferencing: If your class is conferencing online, the following activities in this unit provide good opportunities for online conferencing.

    Get Set: Brainstorm cultural differences online.
    Get Real: Brainstorm supporting sentences online.

    Brainstorming online gives all members of the class the opportunity to share their ideas, even those too shy to speak up in class. (Teachers, read Connecting to the Real World (2) in the To the Teacher section of this book for ideas on using online conferencing.)

Unit 2   What's Up?

Writing about Personal Experiences: Narratives

Sergio:	Hey man, what's up?
Mohammed:	Wanna hear what happened last night?
Sergio:	Sure. What?
Mohammed:	Well, ya know that guy named Shinji in our English class?
Sergio:	Yeah, I know him.
Mohammed:	Well, he . . .

What's up means_____

Get the Picture

Look at the following picture sequence and write a sentence or two for each picture
that tells the story in words. After you have written a sentence or two for each picture,
exchange your sentences with a partner and compare ideas. Does your interpretation
of the story agree with your partner's?

Give-and-Take

The following sentences are taken from a Colombian student's writing journal. The sentences have been scrambled so that the story no longer makes any sense. First decide which sentence is the topic sentence and write it on a separate sheet of paper. Then write the rest of the sentences in the order that makes the most sense to you. Look for a logical progression of ideas. There may be more than one way to unscramble the story. Be sure to use paragraph form. Be prepared to discuss your choices with the rest of the class.

- You can imagine my surprise when during the bumpy ride, a woman set her hibachi in the aisle, put heated coals in the hibachi, and began to cook arepas, a type of flat bread.
- The bus driver was an older man who allowed passengers to board with live chickens and even a hibachi.
- One time when I was a teenager in my native country of Colombia, I took a third-class bus from the tiny town of La Ceja to the big city of Medellín.
- None of this activity seemed to bother the bus driver, who seemed to know the owner of the hibachi well.
- Riding the buses in Colombia is often an unexpected adventure.
- In fact, they might even have been business partners.
- Everyone on the bus began buying the arepas, and soon, people began cranking up the *musica tropical* on their radios.

Go for It

The following stories were written by students in the California State University system and were published in a book called *L.A. Stories: The Voices of Cultural Diversity* by Carol Clark Ottesen (Intercultural Press, 1993. Used with permission of the author). Read the students' narratives.

My Cardboard House

by Erlinda Loriega

Back in Manila, where I grew up, my family was very poor. We lived in a very bad house, partly cardboard. My father was an industrious salesman who tried desperately to make enough commission for Christmas because we had no money.

On Christmas Eve, my father finally got a commission, and he took the bus home from work and seated himself at the back. A man beside him asked for a match for his cigarette. My father reached in his pocket for the match but instead out came his money in an envelope. The money scattered all over and as he tried to pick it up, two men stopped him. They told my father they wanted his money. My father refused. But the bus was crowded and no one cared what was going on. Everyone was afraid, even the bus driver. Those men took all my father's money and beat him up. He thought he could beat those two skinny men in a fight, but they have gangs on the bus and they beat my father like a boxing bag.

It was amazing that my father was able to get home. His face was badly bruised, his ribs cracked and he couldn't work for six months.

The next day was Christmas. That year we had nothing. We settled down with hot coffee and bread. And it was all right because we cared more about taking care of my father. We closed down our door the whole day so the neighbors wouldn't suspect anything. We were also scared. That night about ten o'clock, there was a knock on the door. My mother hesitated to open it, but the knock persisted and my Mom opened it. There was a man who knew my dad. He gave my mom fifty pesos for his debt with my dad. Right away, my mom left for the open market to buy us food. We said our prayers in thankfulness. The great significance of this was the hope it gave us. I truly believe there's hope everywhere, especially now that I am here in the land of the free and bountiful.

Polka-Dot Family

by Michael Haggood

I have had a unique life, straddling two cultures. My father is black and my mother is a blond from Switzerland, so we have what you might call a "Polka-Dot Family." My two sisters and I are black and my brother is not only white but has blond hair. . . . I have experienced black culture for the most part because usually what you look like is what you identify with.

In about 1966, my father had a rare day off and decided to take all of us to Ventura Beach. Mother sent us off with old plastic containers and spoons and we were so happy with the anticipation of getting out of the hot city for a day. We were on Pacific Coast Highway in Malibu when we saw a police car behind us. My dad didn't pay much attention because we weren't doing anything wrong.

Then all of a sudden there were two police cars with lights and sirens on who motioned us to the side of the highway. I remember they yelled at my father to get out and when he did, they slapped handcuffs on him, searched him and kicked him to the ground.

We were scared and crying, not knowing what to do. The officers put him in the police car and put us in the other and drove to the police station. They put him in jail and started to quiz us. They accused my father of kidnapping white children and trying to make his getaway. My mother came down to get us, but still my father had to stay in jail three days until his name was cleared. . . . We were scared, maybe a little bitter, but sometimes we laugh about it now. . . .

I believe being a part of two cultures has been a great asset in my life. Though I have had challenges to overcome, I understand both sides and want to preserve what is best in each one. I am proud to be black and proud to be white, but most of all I want to be a good human being.

Work It Out

A. The following diagram shows how most narratives are developed in English. The description following the diagram should help you understand the usual pattern. Discuss the pattern with your class.

Setting ──────▸ Plot ──────▸ Climax ──────▸ Resolution ──────▸ Conclusion

Description of a Narrative

Personal stories, or narratives, usually follow a particular pattern in English. They normally start with an introduction where the characters, **setting,** and situation are presented. The introduction arouses the curiosity of the reader or listener and leads into the **plot,** or sequence of events. Descriptive adjectives are used to describe how we were feeling at the time of the event. This draws our reader into the emotion and drama of the event.

If the problem and the feelings of the narrator have not already been stated in the introduction, they are revealed in the telling of the plot. The plot describes the sequence of events that progresses toward the **climax,** which is the highest point of interest.

The climax reveals the truth, the unknown element, or what was funny, exciting, sad, or embarrassing.

Finally come the **resolution** and **conclusion.** The resolution reveals how the problem or situation was resolved. The conclusion quickly ties up the story and leaves the reader or listener feeling satisfied.

B. With a group of your classmates, choose one of the narratives to read again. Which sentence in the narrative you have chosen tells the main idea of the whole story? Underline that sentence. On the time chart that follows, write down the setting and then list the events in the order they occurred (chronological order).

Time Chart

1. The setting (where it happened, when it happened, who was present, etc.)

2. The events
    1st

    2nd

    3rd

    4th

    5th

    6th

3. Look for the sentences that identify the problem or conflict, the climax, and the resolution of the problem and discuss these with your group.

4. Discuss how the author closes the narrative.

5. List some of the memorable details of the narrative.

6. Discuss what you think the author's point or purpose was in telling the narrative. Is the author's point the same as the main idea of the whole story?

Get Ready

Look at the picture. Think about what happened. Imagine that you are the person whose bike has been stolen. Create a setting, add details, and describe what your feelings and thoughts would be in this situation. Write your ideas in the tree diagram that follows. A tree diagram like this one helps a writer to generate ideas and consider detail.

Setting: (time, place, situation, other people, etc.)

Details: (specific and descriptive words, colors, textures, sounds, smells, weather, etc.)

Feelings/Thoughts:

Example:
after chemistry class
on campus
late afternoon
no one else in sight. . .

Your ideas

my brand-new mountain bike
beautiful weather, not a cloud
 in the sky
the smell of spring. . .

angry
ripped off
had planned to go
 biking after class at
 Oak Creek. . .

Use the information from your tree diagram to write a narrative on a separate sheet of paper. Follow narrative form with an introduction and a problem (plot), climax, resolution, and conclusion. Remember to make your narrative vivid by including descriptors and details to help bring the story to life for the reader. When you finish, give your paper to your teacher.

Get Set

Use the cluster diagram to brainstorm some of your own memories that you might like to write a narrative about.

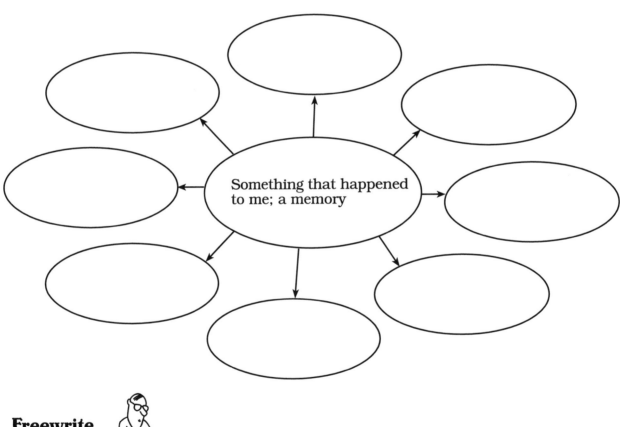

Something that happened to me; a memory

Freewrite

Choose one of your memories and spend 10 minutes writing about it on a separate sheet of paper. Try to write without stopping. Doing a freewrite exercise helps writers formulate ideas. It is a useful tool when you find you are having trouble getting your ideas down on paper. Keep this freewrite exercise for later use.

Get Going

Choose one memory from the ones you came up with in the cluster diagram. Organize your thoughts about this memory by making a tree diagram, a time line, or a time chart about the event. This will help you when it comes time to put your memory into narrative form in the next exercise.

Remember that narratives in English usually follow a pattern of describing the setting and sequence of events, revealing the problem or conflict, describing how the problem or conflict was resolved, and finally bringing the story to a close with a brief and satisfying conclusion.

Setting ⟶ Plot ⟶ Climax ⟶ Resolution ⟶ Conclusion

Remember to include vivid details and to describe how you were feeling to bring your story to life for the reader.

Pull It Together

So far in this unit,

- you have read other writers' narratives;
- you have analyzed narratives and re-created the time lines for them;
- you have used a tree diagram to generate ideas and interesting details for a narrative;
- you have filled in a cluster diagram and completed a freewrite exercise about a memory;
- you have organized your thoughts by making a tree diagram, time line, or time chart in preparation for writing a narrative about a memory of your own.

Now write your memory in narrative form. Use the ideas and details you have gathered to bring your narrative to life through your writing. Write your narrative so that the person reading it will have a strong reaction to your thoughts and ideas. One of your classmates will be reading your narrative. Write with this audience in mind. Remember to have a topic sentence and supporting sentences for each paragraph.

Just Do It

Exchange your narrative with a classmate. Read your classmate's narrative. Now choose sentences that stand out in your mind and write your reaction in the space provided in your classmate's book. You might agree or disagree with your classmate's ideas; you might ask for more detail; you might express an emotion that your class-mate's writing evokes; you might ask about something that wasn't clear to you. This activity is called a **double-entry response.** The purpose is for you to focus your thoughts and feelings about something you have read and, in doing so, aid the writer in revising his or her draft.

The Sentences I Chose Are	*My Reaction Is*

Now hand your classmate's narrative, along with your written reaction, back to your classmate. After reading your classmate's comments, revise your first draft by making any changes you wish to make to your own paper.

Evaluate Yourself

Name _____

Reread the narrative that you wrote and fill in the following form.

1. My narrative includes a topic sentence that tells the main idea of the whole story. The sentence is

2. The topic sentence in each paragraph is easily recognizable.
    __ yes   __ no

    If you answered no, identify the paragraphs that need clear topic sentences and write the topic sentences here.

3. Every sentence in each paragraph relates directly to my topic.
    __ yes   __ no

    If you answered no, identify the sentences that do not directly relate to your topic. Decide whether these sentences need to be rewritten to better clarify your topic or whether you can simply delete them from your paragraph.

4. My narrative follows the pattern of setting, problem or conflict (plot), climax, resolution, and conclusion.
    __ yes   __ no

    If no, what pattern does it follow?

5. My conclusion supports and sums up the main point of my narrative.
    __ yes   __ no

6. I'm having trouble with

    Using your answers on this form as a guide, make any changes you wish to make to your narrative. Now give the original draft, your revisions, the final draft of your narrative, and this self-evaluation to your teacher.

Teacher Feedback

Student's Name _____

Structure

1. Check one.

   __ a. Your narrative flows smoothly and follows a logical order. All of your sentences relate directly to your topic.

   __ b. Your narrative flows less smoothly because it

       __ 1) skips around or goes off topic in one place

       _____

       _____

       __ 2) includes unnecessary information.

       _____

       _____

   __ c. Your narrative does not flow smoothly.

       __ 1) It does not follow a logical order.

       __ 2) It skips around and goes off topic in the following places.

       _____

       _____

       __ 3) It includes the following unnecessary information.

       _____

       _____

2. Your conclusion sums up the main point of your narrative.

   __ yes   __ no

3. Your narrative uses enough descriptive details.

   __ yes   __ no

4. One grammar structure that you seem to be having difficulty with is

Content

1. What I find most interesting about your paper is

2. What I'd like to know more about is

3. Other comments

Live and Learn

Additional Activities and Journal Assignments

1. Work with your teacher and classmates to compile a booklet of your narratives. Make a copy for each member of your class to have as a memento. You might also make a copy to share with a group of native speakers.

2a. Reread the story "My Cardboard House" by Erlinda Loriega in this unit. Check each paragraph for good paragraph form: Does each paragraph have a topic sentence? Do all of the sentences relate directly to the topic sentence? Are there enough supporting sentences to make the topic clear to the reader? Are the sentences in good order? What pattern does the paragraph follow? What are the strengths of this narrative?

2b. Answer the same questions about "Polka-Dot Family" by Michael Haggood.

3. Write a chain narrative with your classmates. Form two or three groups if the class is large. Choose one of the following topics to write the narrative about, or the group can come up with its own topic. Then brainstorm a sentence that will give the main idea of the story. Write this on a piece of paper, an overhead transparency, or a chalkboard. Now each student will add to the narrative in turn. This can be done aloud and written on the board, or it can be done by passing the paper or transparency around to each student in the group, one by one, for a surprise narrative to be read at the end. The first person will begin the story by setting the scene and by introducing the character(s) and the situation of the story in writing. Then each person in turn will add to the story. Each addition to the story must connect logically and sequentially to the previous sentences. They should relate directly to the topic. The last person will bring the story to a logical conclusion. Use descriptive language to make the story interesting and vivid.

    Topic Ideas for a Chain Narrative
      a memorable New Year's celebration
      my first experience with my host family's pet
      the time I was offered an alcoholic drink although I don't drink alcohol
      eating North American food
      my first shopping experience
      my first trip with my host family
      your own ideas

4. Choose a comic strip from a newspaper or magazine. Write a narrative of the comic strip by taking the perspective of one of the characters in the strip. Make a tree diagram, time line, or time chart to help you get started. Be sure to set the scene by describing the setting and the characters involved. Include a sentence that tells the main idea of the whole story. After you've written the narrative from the perspective of one character, choose another character in the strip and write a narrative about the same situation from this character's perspective or have a classmate write from another character's perspective and compare your narratives.

5. As a class, choose one or two of the class narratives to write up as movie scripts. Make a time line or time chart to help you organize the film. Add sketches to the time line to create a storyboard. Write dialogue for each frame in the storyboard. Then film the narratives. Students will take the roles of director, camera operator, actors, and so on. Rehearse before putting your presentation on film. Invite other students, friends, and teachers to view the film.

6. In your journal, describe what you have learned about writing while doing this unit.

7. Online Conferencing: The following activities in this unit provide good opportunities for online conferencing.

   Go for It: Share reactions to the student narratives.
   Get Set: Brainstorm online.
   Live and Learn #3: Write a chain narrative online.

Unit 3   Awesome Performers

Writing Summaries

Awesome performers are _____

Get the Picture

Pop and Opera Come Together

Italian tenor Andrea Bocelli was born in Tuscany, Italy, in 1958 with a visual defect. After a soccer accident at age 12, he lost his sight completely. Bocelli insists that blindness was no tragedy for him. In the May 19, 1997, edition of the British newspaper the *Independent,* Bocelli is quoted as saying, "The tragedy is that people continue to make a fuss out of something which they consider tragic, not I." About his blindness he says, "Everyone has problems to overcome. The important thing is to overcome them and not to create more of them for yourself." Certainly, his blindness has not adversely affected his career.

Educated as a lawyer but with an unmistakable talent in music, Andrea Bocelli is in the unique position of being adored by fans of both pop music and classical opera. He has taken master classes with tenor Luciano Pavarotti and has sung for the pope. Long popular in his home country of Italy, he became a hit with the British in 1996 after recording "Time to Say Good-bye" (Con Te Partiro) with British singer Sarah Brightman.

The song was originally recorded as a solo by Bocelli. Brightman apparently heard it while dining out, was enchanted by it, and tracked down Bocelli. The two of them rerecorded it as a duet with the London Symphony Orchestra. Brightman and Bocelli performed the song in Germany at the retirement fight of German light-heavyweight champion Henry Maske. The crowd responded enthusiastically. Maske was moved to tears. "Con Te Partiro" became the biggest selling single of all time in Germany with sales of nearly three million copies.

Bocelli has been number one on the pop music charts in Germany, Austria, Belgium, the Netherlands, France, and Switzerland. Both his classical and pop music became popular in North America after a PBS special featured Bocelli performing both kinds of music. Bocelli enjoys the opportunities to sing pop music but prefers singing classical music. In an interview with Victoria White of the *Irish Times* he states, "I like opera more than anything else."

Scan the reading for the answers to the following questions. Answer the questions using complete sentences.

1. Who is Andrea Bocelli?

2. Has Bocelli's blindness been a tragedy for him?

3. What kind of music does he perform?

4. Where is his music popular?

5. According to an article in the *Irish Times*, what kind of music does Bocelli prefer?

Give-and-Take

Work in small groups to complete this exercise.
1. Using your answers to the scan questions, make a list of the most important points from this article.

2. Finish the following sentence.

   The purpose of scan questions is _____

   _____

Go for It

Read the following article about Madonna.

Madonna's Climb to the Top

Pop culture phenomenon Madonna began her climb to the top in New York City with just $35 in her pocket. Madonna Louise Veronica Ciccone was born in 1958 in Michigan. Her mother died of cancer when she was six. Her father remarried two years later, but Madonna never got along well with her stepmother. Madonna was the eldest daughter of eight children in the combined family. She wasn't very happy growing up in her family. As she got older she felt as if she had to stand up for herself and make a strong impression on others.

A cheerleader in high school, Madonna also studied piano and ballet. She earned a scholarship to study dance at the University of Michigan but dropped out after two years to move to New York. Her goal was to take New York City by storm.

She wanted to perform the kind of music she liked best—Stevie Wonder, the Supremes, Marvin Gaye. She liked the pop songs of the 1960s, calling them innocent little songs. She didn't like hard rock, heavy metal, or jazz. Pop and soul were her favorites. Madonna wanted to make music that she could dance to. A record deal with Sire Records made this dream come true.

Music videos, an original style, and a drive to make it big took her to the top. She has been dubbed *the* pop music figure of the eighties and nineties, and it doesn't look as though she has any plans to slow down.

Now complete the following tasks.

1. Identify and discuss the main ideas of this article with your classmates.

2. On your own, write scan questions that identify these main points.

3. Exchange your scan questions with a classmate. Do you and your classmate agree on the most important points in this article? Discuss any points of disagreement and make changes to your questions.

4. Now put the main ideas in order. Explain why you have chosen to put them in this order.

Work It Out

Description of a Summary

Writing scan questions and answering them is one way to prepare to write a summary. Think about the kind of information the scan questions and answers provide about an article.

Working with a small group, answer the following questions about summaries. Your answers to these questions should provide you with some guidelines to writing summaries. Be prepared to share your answers with the class.

1. What kind of information from the article do you think is in a summary?

2. What is not included in a summary?

3. In what order is the information in a summary presented?

4. How long is a summary?

5. How does the process of writing and answering scan questions help you in writing a summary?

Get Real

A. Read the following guidelines for writing a summary. Did your group arrive at the same guidelines? Discuss any differences with your teacher and classmates. What would you add to or omit from these guidelines? Why?

Guidelines for Writing a Summary

1. State the source and title of the article you are summarizing. For example, in a summary of the article about Andrea Bocelli you might write the following.

    According to the article "Pop and Opera Come Together" in *Write about It!* Andrea Bocelli has never considered his blindness a problem.

2. Include only information from the reading, graph, chart, or survey that is important. *Don't* include unimportant details. *Do* include all of the major points.

3. Include a sentence that tells the main idea of the whole article or chart. Report the main ideas and major points of the article accurately.

4. Use your own words, not those of the author. If you do use the author's words, you must put quotation marks around them. For example: According to an article in *Write about It!* "Pop culture phenomenon Madonna began her climb to the top in New York City with just $35 in her pocket."

5. Avoid giving your personal opinions.

6. Present the important information in a logical order. If you are summarizing a chart or survey, arrange the data in an order that will make it easy for the reader to understand the information. If you are summarizing an article, arrange the information in the order the author presents it or other logical order.

7. Remember that a summary of a reading is shorter than the original reading. It is often only one-third the length of the original article.

B. Using these guidelines and your answers to your scan questions, write a summary of the reading about Madonna. Write for an audience who may not know who Madonna is.

Pull It Together

So far in this unit,

*   you have read articles and created scan questions and answers for the articles;
*   you have discussed the use of scan questions in writing summaries;
*   you have analyzed the components of a summary and created guidelines for writing summaries;
*   you have written one summary.

Now, write another summary. Follow the steps listed here.

1. Find an article or a chart related to the topic of entertainment. You can look in the entertainment sections of magazines and newspapers or on the Internet.
2. Read the article or chart and write scan questions for it.
3. Answer the questions and make a list of the major points.
4. Put the information in a logical order.
5. Use your answers and your list and the Guidelines for Writing a Summary to help you write a summary about your article or chart. Remember to have a topic sentence and supporting sentences for each paragraph. When you have finished writing your summary, you will be giving it to a classmate. This person will not be familiar with the information in the article or chart and may not be familiar with the topic you've chosen to write about. Write with this audience in mind.
6. When you have finished writing your summary, go to Polish It in the Appendix at the back of this book. Use the checklist to help you look for grammatical and mechanical problems in your summary.

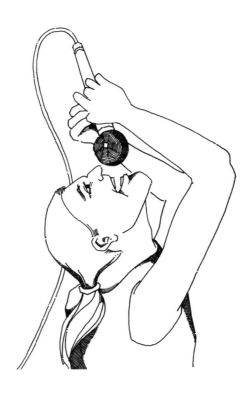

Just Do It

A. Exchange summaries with a classmate. Read your classmate's summary and write scan questions for it. Then return your classmate's summary along with your questions to your classmate.

B. Read the scan questions your classmate wrote for your summary. Compare the scan questions you wrote with the ones your classmate came up with. Are they different? If so, you may need to reread your article and your summary to make sure you have included the most important points from the article.

C. Revise your first draft by making any changes you want to make to your summary. Then complete the self-evaluation that follows.

Evaluate Yourself Name _____

Reread the summary that you wrote and fill in the following form.

1. The title and source of my article or chart are stated in my summary.
    __ yes __ no
2. My summary includes a sentence that tells the main idea of the whole article or chart. The sentence is

3. My summary includes the answers to all of my scan questions.
    __ yes __ no

    If no, which answers are not included and why?

4. My summary is written in my own words. I have used quotation marks when using the exact words from the article.
    __ yes __ no
5. My summary does *not* include my opinion.
    __ yes __ no
6. The information in my summary is arranged in a logical order. Circle one.

    a. It follows the arrangement of information in the chart.
    b. It follows the order in which the author presents the information in the article.
    c. Other (identify)

7. I reported the information from the chart or article accurately in my summary.
    __ yes __ no
8. I'm having trouble with

Using your answers on this form as a guide, make any changes you wish to make to your summary. Now give the original article or chart, your scan questions and answers, the original draft of your summary, revised drafts, the final draft of your summary, and this self-evaluation to your teacher.

Teacher Feedback

Student's Name _____

Structure

1. The title and source of your article or chart are mentioned in your summary.
   __ yes   __ no

2. Your paper includes a sentence that tells the main idea of the whole paper. The sentence is

3. Your summary presents the information in a logical order.
   __ yes   __ no

   If not, the problem is

4. Check one.

   __ a. You have written the summary in your own words.
   __ b. You have used the words of the author without quotation marks. (See the underlined sentences in your summary.)

5. One grammar structure that you seem to be having difficulty with is

Content

1. You included *only* important information from the chart or article.
   __ yes   __ no

   If not, the problem is

2. You reported the information from the chart or article accurately in your summary.
   __ yes   __ no

   If not, the problem is

3. You included all of the major points.

___ yes ___ no

If not, you left out the following points.

4. ___ You did not include your personal opinion.
___ You included your personal opinion in the following place(s).

5. What I find most interesting about your paper is

Other comments

Live and Learn

Additional Activities and Journal Assignments

1. As a class, see a movie together. Then, as a group, write scan questions and answers and list the major points. Write a summary of the movie. Share the summary in an in-house newsletter or a campus newspaper or post it on a bulletin board or an in-house web page. After the summary is written, you might also get a show of hands as to whether this is a movie the class would recommend that others see or not and post that information as well. (If you plan to show a film or video in the classroom, you should first check with your institution to find out the established policies for using copyrighted material in the classroom.)

2. Choose an article or a chart on a topic other than entertainment to write a summary about. It can be about any topic you are interested in. You can find poll results on a variety of topics on the Internet. Write scan questions and answers and/or list the major points of the article to prepare for writing the summary. Then write the summary.

3. In your journal, write a letter to a friend that summarizes one of your favorite books or a favorite film. List the major points to help get you started.

4. In your journal, write a letter to a friend or relative that summarizes your experiences here in the last few months. This is not a narrative but a summary. How will it differ from a narrative?

5. As a class, design and take a poll about music preferences among your peers or about any other topic you are interested in. Study the results of your poll, present your findings in a chart, and write a summary about your findings. Share this information in an in-house newsletter or a campus newspaper, on a bulletin board, or on an in-house web page.

Topic Ideas for a Poll or Survey
   recycling habits
   restaurant preferences
   TV viewing habits
   career objectives
   top 10 greatest athletes
   leisure time activities

6. In your journal, describe what you have learned about writing while doing this unit.

7. Online Conferencing: The following activities in this unit provide good opportunities for online conferencing.

Give-and-Take: Answer questions 1 and 2 online.

Go for It: Answer questions 1, 2, and 3 online.

Live and Learn #1: Share opinions about the movie online.

Live and Learn #5: Poll each other online.

Unit 4　Climbing the Corporate Ladder

Summarizing and Reacting

Climbing the corporate ladder means _____

Get the Picture

Read the following scrambled dialogue from the comic strip *Dilbert* by Scott Adams. After discussing unfamiliar vocabulary in the dialogue, match the dialogue to the pictures and write the correct sentences for each frame of the strip on the lines provided.

A.   It must be hard to remain motivated when you know you can never break through the glass ceiling.
B.   So, it looks like it's just tile after all.
C.   I admire your work ethic, Alice. You're even working during your vacation.

"Dilbert" © 1997 United Feature Syndicate. Reprinted by permission.

1. _____   2. _____   3. _____

_____   _____   _____

_____   _____   _____

_____   _____   _____

Answer the following questions.

1.   What is the man surprised about?

2.   The "glass ceiling" is the expression used to describe how difficult it is for qualified women to gain top corporate positions. Would the man be affected by a glass ceiling?

3.   What is Alice's response to the man's concerns?

Get Set

Look up the word *sexism* in your dictionary. Brainstorm examples of behaviors that you have observed to be sexist. You might have observed them in your own culture, or you might have observed them in this country. You may have observed them in movies, in advertisements, or in real life.

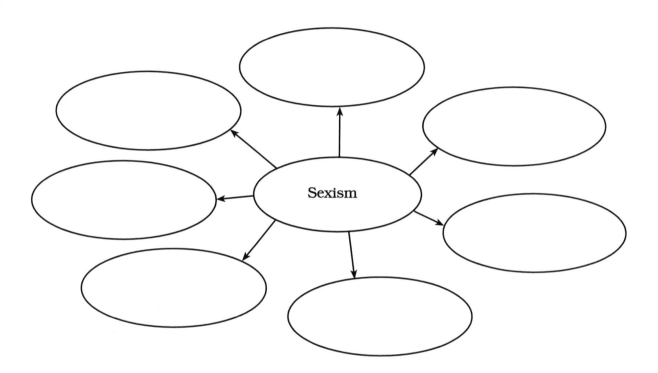

Discuss your ideas with your classmates and add any new ideas to your cluster diagram.

Freewrite

Choose one of the sexist behaviors you and your classmates came up with and spend 10 minutes writing about it on a separate sheet of paper. Try to write without stopping. Keep this freewrite exercise for later use.

Get Ready

There are three important categories of behavior covered in this unit: sexist actions, sexual discrimination, and sexual harassment. Sexist actions include any actions or language that demean women or identify women as less important members of the workforce. Sexual discrimination means a refusal to hire or to promote someone based solely on the person's gender. Sexual harassment is deliberate or repeated sexual behavior that is unwelcome and not returned. It can be verbal, such as sexual comments or jokes, nonverbal, such as leering looks, or physical, such as inappropriate touching. When this behavior affects the working environment, work performance, promotions, pay, or other working conditions, it is illegal. Legally, sexual harassment is considered a form of discrimination.

Following are eight different situations. Read each one and decide whether it is sexist action, sexual discrimination, or sexual harassment. Write the number of the situation in the appropriate category.

Sexist Actions	Sexual Discrimination	Sexual Harassment

1. An employee repeatedly uses e-mail to send sexual jokes to other staff members even after being told not to.
2. A female sales representative asks a male employee at a factory for dates whenever she makes a sales call, and he keeps telling her, "No."
3. A female employee makes unwelcome sexual comments to a male coworker at an office party after work hours.
4. A male employee frequently brushes up against female employees. He says it's accidental, but the women don't believe him.

5. An employer decides to hire a man to pick up the garbage because he doesn't think that the woman who applied should be doing that kind of work.

6. After a successful business transaction, a male supervisor compliments his female employees and gives all of the men in the office a 10 percent raise.

7. A cashier in a coffee shop in the building greets customers by calling them "honey" or "dearie."

8. Before a staff meeting, a male manager says to two female secretaries, "Why don't you two girls get us some coffee?"

Get Real

You have categorized eight situations as sexist action, sexual discrimination, or sexual harassment. Do any of these situations make you feel angry, sad, discouraged, helpless, confused, or unimportant? Try to put yourself in the position of a person in one of these situations. Choose the situation from among these eight that causes the strongest reaction in you. On a separate piece of paper, write a one-paragraph reaction. Remember to include a topic sentence and supporting sentences.

Go for It

Understanding What You Read

A. Read the composition "What's the Big Deal?" Read the entire composition without stopping.

What's the Big Deal?

Both women and men face many obstacles as they compete for the best jobs in the workplace. One of these obstacles is the traditional attitude that women are the "home-makers" and men are the "breadwinners." This attitude reflects the belief that men are superior to women and women are subordinate to men. This attitude is called **sexism.** It is an attitude that denies equal opportunities for all and affects the working environment in the areas of work performance, promotions, pay, and working conditions.

The language associated with this attitude is called **sexist.** Historically, men have been in the position of power, so sexist language is usually directed at women. Sexist vocabulary is used to demean women, to identify them as less important members of the workforce. For example, at the end of a staff meeting, a male manager says to two female secretaries, "Why don't you two girls clean up this room?" Referring to mature women as "girls" is demeaning; it infers that they are not capable of handling difficult problems or situations. It is also sexist to use terms of endearment such as "honey," "sweetie," or "dear" when speaking to employees or coworkers, or to make casual comments about a woman's physical looks or what she is wearing.

Sexist attitudes are often displayed in nonverbal ways through inappropriate actions such as telling jokes or showing cartoons that portray men as superior. Expectations by male bosses that a woman should be responsible for making coffee or tea for the office staff or be in charge of planning and arranging a business social event are also examples of sexist attitudes. All of these actions are considered sexist behavior.

As more and more women have joined the workforce, there has been increased pressure to change our attitudes. One of the changes has been in the language we use. For example, the man or woman who delivers our mail is now called a mail carrier, and instead of saying "salesgirl" for the female clerk in a department store, we say, "salesclerk." These changes in language reflect the attempt to eliminate sexist attitudes from our society.

More pressure to change our attitudes and behaviors has come from the legislature of the United States. Laws have been passed that prohibit both discrimination based on sex and sexual harassment. According to the Civil Rights Act of 1964, it is illegal in the United States to refuse to hire or to discriminate against someone based on sex. For example, if an employer decides to hire a man to pick up the garbage because the employer doesn't think women should be doing that kind of work, it is discrimination based on gender, and it is illegal.

It is also illegal to sexually harass anyone at the workplace. Legal experts define sexual harassment as deliberate or repeated sexual behavior that is unwelcome and not returned. It can be verbal, such as sexual comments or jokes, nonverbal, such as leering looks, or physical, such as inappropriate touching. When this behavior affects the working environment, work performance, promotions, pay, or other working conditions, it is illegal. If a male employee frequently brushes up against female employees "accidentally," this is sexual harassment, and it is illegal. An employee who repeatedly uses e-mail to send sexual jokes to other staff members even after being told not to is guilty of sexual harassment, and legal action can be taken against this person and against the company for not putting a stop to this behavior.

Sexual harassment is a big deal to the employees involved and to the companies they work for. It is not a laughing matter; it is a serious problem that has cost companies millions of dollars spent on lawsuits brought by both men and women. Between 1991 and 1997, companies in the United States paid $49.7 million dollars in sexual harassment complaints, according to the Equal Employment Opportunity Commission (EEOC). The number of sexual harassment charges brought by both men and women doubled during the same period of time. This increase in legal complaints is not due to more sexual harassment taking place on the job but to a greater awareness of the problem and the willingness of employees to speak up.

In the past, sexist attitudes helped to create a work environment where both sexual discrimination and sexual harassment were tolerated. Employees feared for both their personal security and their job security. Today's workers, however, are better informed about their legal rights and are more likely to challenge sexism, sexual discrimination, and sexual harassment by employers or coworkers.

B. Read "What's the Big Deal?" again and circle or underline words that are causing confusion. Try to understand them from the context. It is important to try to define new words by looking at the context in which they were written. Reread the sentences that come before or after the sentence containing an unfamiliar word. Carefully read the words or phrases surrounding the new word. Often these sentences or phrases contain clues to the meaning of the new word.

C. Finally, if there are places in the reading that you simply cannot understand, use your dictionary as an aid. But remember, you don't need to understand every word in the reading to understand the main points.

Work It Out

Making a chart helps a reader to understand an article and helps a writer to organize information. A chart can help define the subtopics and the kind of support given for each subtopic of an article. Work with a partner to analyze the reading by completing the following chart. Share your completed chart with the class.

The main topic of the whole article is _____

Subtopics	Definition	Support from the Reading	My Reactions
Sexism (Sexist action or language)			
Sexual discrimination			
Sexual harassment			

Pull It Together

So far in this unit,

- you have completed a freewrite exercise about sexism;
- you have learned to distinguish the differences among sexism, sexual discrimination, and sexual harassment;

- you have written your reaction to a situation involving sexism, sexual discrimination, or sexual harassment;
- you have read an article and used a chart to analyze and react to the article.

Now, write a reaction paper by summarizing the article and your reactions to it. Look at the suggestions that follow to help you in writing your paper.

1. Look back at the freewrite exercise you completed earlier and at the reaction you wrote about a particular sexist behavior to help you get started. The chart in Work It Out can help you to organize your thoughts and your paper. Since this is a reaction paper rather than a summary, you will want to connect the ideas raised in the reading to your own thoughts and experiences.

2. You may want to write scan questions and answers or list the major points of the article to further help you organize your ideas.

3. You may want to look back at the Guidelines for Writing a Summary in Unit 3. The difference between a reaction paper and a summary is that in a reaction paper you may include your opinion or reaction.

4. Remember to have a topic sentence and supporting sentences for each of your paragraphs.

5. When you have finished writing your reaction paper, go to Polish It in the Appendix at the back of this book. Use the editing checklist to help you look for grammatical and mechanical problems in your paper.

Just Do It

Exchange your reaction paper with a classmate. Read your classmate's paper. Now choose sentences that stand out in your mind and write your reaction in the space provided in your classmate's book. You might agree or disagree with your classmate's ideas; you might ask for more detail; you might express an emotion that your classmate's writing evokes; you might ask about something that wasn't clear to you. This activity is called a **double-entry response.** The purpose is for you to focus your thoughts and feelings about something you have read and, in doing so, aid the writer in revising his or her draft.

The sentences I chose are	My reaction is

Now hand your classmate's paper, along with your written reaction, back to your classmate. After reading your classmate's comments, make any changes you wish to make to the first draft of your paper.

Evaluate Yourself

Name _____

Reread the reaction paper that you wrote and fill in the following form.

1. The title and source of my article are stated in my reaction paper.
   __ yes   __ no
2. My paper includes a sentence that tells the main idea. The sentence is

3. My paper includes definitions and other support such as examples or statistics to support each topic sentence.
   __ yes   __ no
4. My paper includes my reactions to the issue.
   __ yes   __ no
5. My paper is written in my own words. I have used quotation marks when using the exact words from the article.
   __ yes   __ no
6. I have included all of the major points from the article in my paper.
   __ yes   __ no
7. The information in my paper is organized clearly.
   __ yes   __ no

   (Show how you have organized your paper here.)

8. I'm having trouble with

Using your answers on this form as a guide, revise your paper as needed. Now give your chart, your scan questions and answers if you wrote them, the original draft of your paper, revised drafts, the final draft of your paper, and this self-evaluation to your teacher.

Teacher Feedback

Student's Name _____

Structure

1. The title and source of your article are mentioned in your reaction paper.
   __ yes   __ no

2. Your paper includes a sentence that tells the main idea of the whole paper. The sentence is

3. Your paper presents the information in a logical order.
   __ yes   __ no

   If not, the problem is

4. Check one.

   __ a. You have written the paper in your own words.
   __ b. You have used the words of the author without quotation marks. (See the underlined sentences in your paper.)

5. One grammar structure that you seem to be having difficulty with is

Content

1. Your paper includes definitions and other support such as examples or explanations to support each topic sentence.
   __ yes   __ no

2. You included *only* important information from the article.
   __ yes   __ no

   If not, the problem is

3. You reported the information from the article accurately in your paper.
   __ yes   __ no

   If not, the problem is

4. You included all of the major points.
   __ yes   __ no

   If not, you left out the following points.

5. You included your reaction to the issues raised in the article.
   __ yes   __ no

6. What I find most interesting about your paper is

7. Other comments

Live and Learn

Additional Activities and Journal Assignments

1. Look in newspapers for articles on sexual discrimination and sexual harassment. Bring them to class to share. After sharing, choose one of the articles to write a reaction to. Remember to summarize the article and include your reaction or opinion. Charts, scan questions, and lists of major points can help you organize your paper.

2. Look for advertisements, comics, cartoons, and songs that you consider sexist. Explain to the class why you consider the material sexist. Then choose one of the examples and write a reaction to it. Remember to summarize the content and include your reaction or opinion. Charts, scan questions, and lists of major points can help you organize your paper.

3. Read letters to the editor in your local or campus newspaper about a controversial issue. Identify the author's main points in one of these letters and write your reactions in a letter of your own. Remember to summarize the letter and include your reaction or opinion. Charts, scan questions, and lists of major points can help you organize your paper.

4. Find an article about your own country or culture and write a reaction paper to it. Remember to summarize the article and include your reaction or opinion. Charts, scan questions, and lists of major points can help you organize your paper.

5. Have an affirmative action officer from a school or business in your community come and speak to your class. The class can prepare questions based on what they have learned in this unit. Afterward, you can summarize the information from the talk and write your reactions to it.

6. As a class, watch popular films, such as "Disclosure" that address the issues of sexism, sexual discrimination or sexual harassment or that have scenes depicting any of these behaviors. Afterward, summarize and write a reaction to the films or the scenes. Before you present a film, video recording, or TV excerpt, you should check with your institution to find out the established policies for using copyrighted material of this kind.

7. In your journal, describe what you have learned about writing while doing this unit.

8. Online Conferencing: The following activities in this unit provide good opportunities for online conferencing.

Get Set: Brainstorm online.

Get Ready: Teachers: post the eight situations online. Students: review the eight situations your teacher has posted online. Put them into categories and post your choices. Share your reasons with your classmates.

Live and Learn #3: Teachers: post a letter to the editor from your local or campus newspaper online. Students: read the letter to the editor that your teacher has posted online. Share your reactions with your classmates online.

Unit 5 Getting Popped for Being Bombed behind the Wheel

Preparing to Write a Research Paper: Outlining

Getting popped for being bombed behind the wheel means

a. drinking a soft drink while driving a car
b. having a bomb thrown at your car while you are driving
c. getting stopped by the police for driving under the influence of alcohol

Get the Picture

This picture is the logo for an organization called MADD, Mothers Against Drunk Driving. (MADD logo used with permission.)

1. What do you think the logo means?

2. Why do you think this organization is called MADD? Do you think only mothers belong to this organization?

3. Is drinking and driving a problem in your country?

4. What are the laws about drinking and driving in your country?

Get Ready

Some important information is missing from this chart on blood alcohol content. Find the missing information in the reading and use it to complete the chart.

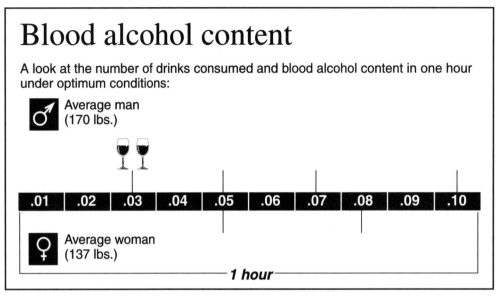

National Highway Traffic Safety Administration

Blood alcohol content (BAC) is used to decide whether it is lawful for a person who has been drinking alcohol to drive. At this time, 34 states in the United States allow a BAC of 0.10 percent, but 16 states have tightened their standards for drunken driving from 0.10 to 0.08 percent. These states are Alabama, California, Florida, Hawaii, Idaho, Illinois, Kansas, Maine, New Hampshire, New Mexico, North Carolina, Oregon, Utah, Vermont, Virginia, and Washington. More states are considering lowering the BAC limits, and some cities within some states have a lower limit.

How many drinks does it take to raise a person's BAC above the legal limits? According to the National Highway Traffic Safety Administration, an average man (weighing 170 lbs) who drinks two alcoholic drinks within one hour will have a BAC of 0.03 percent. If he has three drinks, his BAC rises to 0.05 percent; four drinks send his BAC up to 0.07 percent; and five drinks in one hour raises his BAC to 0.10 percent. On the other hand, an average woman (weighing 137 lbs) has a BAC of 0.05 percent after drinking just two drinks in one hour, and after she has three drinks in one hour, her BAC rises to 0.08 percent.

Now, complete the chart by filling in the number of drinks consumed per hour at the corresponding blood alcohol content. The first one has been done for you.

Some people are opposed to BAC standards. Critics argue that current BAC legal limits make criminals out of social drinkers. Discuss the following questions with your class.

1. What is a social drinker?
2. Do you think a man who has five drinks in one hour or a woman who has three drinks in one hour should be driving a car? Why or why not?

Get Set

Use the following cluster diagram to brainstorm ideas about drinking and driving. Expand it as necessary. What effect does drinking alcohol have on a person's body, and how does drinking affect a person's ability to drive? How does it affect families? What do you know about the issue?

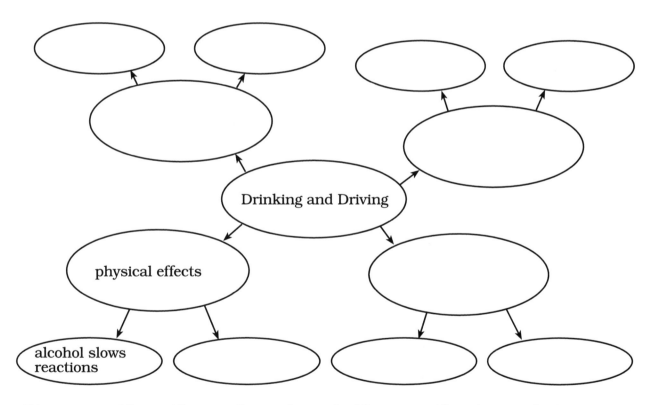

Discuss your ideas with your classmates and add any new ideas to your cluster diagram.

Freewrite

Now choose one or more of the ideas from your cluster diagram and spend 10 minutes writing about them on a separate sheet of paper. Connect the ideas to your own thoughts and experiences. Try to write without stopping. Keep this freewrite exercise for later use.

Go for It

Read the following article about drinking and driving. Use the reading strategies you learned in Unit 4 to help you understand unfamiliar words. After reading the article, you will make an outline that will reveal to you how the writer organized the paper.

The Deadly Duo

The "Deadly Duo," drinking and driving, is the number one cause of death in the United States for people between the ages of 18 and 21.

Effects of Alcohol in the Blood

Any amount of alcohol in the bloodstream impairs the ability to drive. After entering the stomach, alcohol goes quickly to the bloodstream, where it is carried to all parts of the body, including the brain. Alcohol affects those parts of the brain that control coordination, judgment, emotions, and confidence.

Alcohol often gives a driver a false sense of confidence. After drinking, many people feel that they can drive better. They also feel that they can react quickly in an emergency. Of course, this false sense of confidence is the result of alcohol's effect on the brain.

In fact, after drinking, reaction time is slowed, including the time it takes to decide to step on the brake or turn the steering wheel. Coordination is also adversely affected. The ability to brake solidly with the foot and turn accurately is impaired. Vision, especially at night, is affected by alcohol.

How Much Does It Take?

It doesn't take much alcohol to impair driving ability. How much it takes depends on a number of factors. Body weight is one such factor. It will take less alcohol to affect a person who weighs 120 pounds than a person who weighs 180 pounds. It takes less time to get intoxicated on an empty stomach than it does on a full stomach. The alcohol content of a person's drink and how long the person has been drinking are also factors.

Additionally, if a person takes medication or uses drugs in combination with alcohol, driving ability will be greatly impaired.

Blood Alcohol Level

Blood alcohol level is measured through a chemical analysis of the breath (called a Breathalyzer test), or it is measured through a chemical analysis of the blood. The higher the blood alcohol level of a driver, the greater the probability there is of him or her causing an accident. At a blood alcohol level of .20 percent, the probability is over 50 percent. The following chart shows the relationship of body weight, number of drinks, and blood alcohol level.

		Weight in Pounds					
		120	140	160	180	200	220
D	1	.03	.03	.02	.02	.02	.02
R	2	.06	.05	.05	.04	.04	.03
I	3	.09	.08	.07	.06	.06	.05
N	4	.12	.11	.09	.08	.08	.07
K	5	.16	.13	.12	.11	.09	.09
S	6	.19	.16	.14	.13	.11	.10

Blood Alcohol Level

From the American Medical Association.

Currently, in most states it is considered unsafe and illegal to drive if your blood alcohol level is .10 percent or higher in proportion to body weight. In some states the blood alcohol limit is lower. Many states are considering lowering the blood alcohol limit to .08 percent alcohol, and at least one state proposes reducing the limit to .04 percent.

The Consequences of Drunk Driving

If your blood alcohol level is higher than the limit allowed by law, you will be arrested. The consequences of driving while under the influence of intoxicants (DUII) can include heavy fines, jail, or loss of your license for as short a period as three months or as long as three years. Your punishment will depend on the circumstances and whether or not you have a history of drunk driving. In some states refusing to take the Breathalyzer test will result in your having your driver's license taken away. Obviously, the worst consequence of driving drunk is killing an innocent person or becoming one of the almost 20,000 a year alcohol-related traffic deaths yourself—consequences that can never be set right.

Playing It Safe

If you plan to drink, eat before drinking and while drinking. Food slows down how fast alcohol gets into your blood. Drink slowly and space your drinks out over time to keep alcohol from building up in your bloodstream. Order one or two soft drinks, juices, or water after each alcoholic drink. It takes about one hour for the body to rid itself of one drink so stop drinking alcohol at least one hour before you drive. Have coffee, nonalcoholic punch, and dessert instead. Dance and enjoy the party while your body rids itself of alcohol.

Designate a driver, one person in the group who will not drink alcohol and will be the only one allowed to drive. This is a good way to ensure the safety of everyone. Call a taxi if necessary. It's a lot cheaper than a fine or an arrest and conviction for DUII. And more importantly it may save a life. Drinking and driving don't mix. Be a responsible driver. Don't drink and drive.

Work It Out

Look back at the reading. Fill in the outline for the article "The Deadly Duo" to see how the writer has organized the paper. Each section of the outline should include the main idea followed by supporting details such as definitions, examples, facts and statistics, explanations, reasons, and so on. Extend the outline as needed. The first part has been done for you. When you have finished, share your outline with the class.

I. **The Deadly Duo**
   Main Idea: Drinking and driving can be fatal.
   Supporting Details:
   - The "deadly duo" is drinking and driving. *(definition)*
   - Drinking and driving is the number one cause of death in the U.S. for people aged 18 to 21. *(statistics)*

II. **Effects of Alcohol in the Blood**
   Main Idea: Alcohol impairs the ability to drive.
   Supporting Details: *(facts)*
   - Alcohol enters the bloodstream quickly.
   - Alcohol is carried to the brain, where it affects judgment, emotions, and confidence.
   - Alcohol gives a false sense of confidence.

- Alcohol slows reaction time.
  (examples)
    a. It takes longer to decide to step on the brake.
    b. It takes longer to decide to turn the steering wheel.
- Alcohol adversely affects coordination.
  (examples)
    a. Drinkers have trouble braking solidly with the foot.
    b. Drinkers have trouble turning accurately.
- Alcohol affects vision, especially at night.

III. How Much Does It Take?
Main Idea:
Supporting Details:
  -
  -

IV. Blood Alcohol Level
Main Idea:
Supporting Details:
  -
  -

V. The Consequences of Drunk Driving
Main Idea:
Supporting Details:
  -
  -

VI. Playing It Safe
Main Idea:
Supporting Details:
  -
  -

Pull It Together

So far in this unit,

- you have shared ideas about the issue of drinking and driving with your classmates;
- you have analyzed and discussed a chart about blood alcohol level with your classmates;
- you have completed a freewrite exercise about drinking and driving;
- you have used an outline to analyze the organization of an article.

A.   Read the following scenario.

You went to a party last week with a friend. Your friend drove you both to the party in his car. Alcohol was served at the party. You didn't drink any alcohol, but your friend drank a lot. When it came time to go home, you told your friend that you wanted his car keys to drive you both home. He became angry and said he wasn't drunk. You insisted. He was too drunk to resist, so you drove the car home. But, your friend is now very angry with you. He says you overreacted and embarrassed him. He doesn't even want to speak with you anymore. You have been friends for a long time. You don't want this to be the end of your friendship.

B.   Write a letter to your friend explaining why you took his car keys from him. Look at the suggestions that follow to help you in writing your paper.

1. Look back at the freewrite exercise you completed earlier to help you get started.
2. State the main idea or purpose of your letter.
3. Make an outline of the information that you will include in your letter; you may want to include facts from the reading to support your main points. You may want to look back at the outline in this chapter or ask your teacher for help in organizing your outline.
4. Remember to have a topic sentence and supporting sentences for each of your paragraphs.
5. When you have finished writing your letter, go to Polish It in the Appendix at the back of this book. Use the editing checklist to help you look for grammatical and mechanical problems in your letter.

Just Do It

1. Exchange your letter with a classmate. Now each of you will pretend to be the "drunk friend." Read your classmate's letter and think about how you want to respond. Decide whether you want to continue the friendship. On a separate sheet of paper, make a chart or an outline to help you organize your response. Then write your response. Be sure to state your reasons for continuing or discontinuing the friendship.
2. After you have written your response, give your classmate's letter, along with your response, back to your classmate.
3. Now make any changes you wish to make to your own letter.

Evaluate Yourself   Name _____

Reread the letter that you wrote and fill in the following form.

1. My letter includes a sentence that tells the main idea. The sentence is

2. My letter includes information to support my actions.
    __ yes   __ no
3. My letter is written in my own words. I have used quotation marks when using the exact words from the article.
    __ yes   __ no
4. The information in my letter is organized clearly and follows my outline.
    __ yes   __ no
5. I was successful in convincing my friend to remain friends with me.
    __ yes   __ no

    I think the reason I was successful/unsuccessful is

6. I'm having trouble with

Using your answers on this form as a guide, make any changes you wish to make to your letter. Now give your outline, the original draft of your letter, revised drafts, the final draft of your letter, and this self-evaluation to your teacher.

Teacher Feedback

Student's Name _____

Structure

1. Your letter includes a sentence that tells the main idea of the whole letter. The sentence is

2. Your letter presents the information in a logical order.
   __ yes   __ no

   If not, the problem is

3. Check one.

   __ a. You have written the letter in your own words.
   __ b. You have used the exact words from the article without quotation marks. (See the underlined sentences in your letter.)

4. One grammar structure that you seem to be having difficulty with is

Content

1. Your letter includes information such as examples, facts, and statistics to support your actions.
   __ yes   __ no
2. You reported the information from the article accurately in your letter.
   __ yes   __ no

   If not, the problem is

3. What I find most interesting about your letter is

4. Other comments

Live and Learn

Additional Activities and Journal Assignments

1. Look in newspapers for articles on drinking and driving or about alcohol abuse on campuses. Bring them to class to share. After sharing, use the information from the articles to write a paper about the issue. Make an outline to help you organize your paper and remember to use quotation marks when using the exact words from an article.

2. Write for information from MADD, P.O. Box 541688, Dallas, TX 75354–1688, or look up MADD on the Internet. Design your own pamphlet or website about the issue of drinking and driving.

3. Use the Internet to find out more about the different issues surrounding drinking and driving, for example, the drunk driving laws in different states and provinces, the liability of taverns and how they deal with the issue, and Alcoholics Anonymous. Alone or with a partner, write a paper about what you've learned. Make an outline to help you organize your paper.

4. You and your friends are planning a party. Your friends want to serve alcoholic beverages at the party. You are worried that someone may drink too much and then try to drive home. In your journal, write a note to your friends explaining your feelings and what actions you think you and your friends should take to make sure no one tries to drive home drunk. Make an outline to help you organize your paper.

5. In your journal write about the issue of social drinking. What is social drinking? How much alcohol intake should be considered social, and how much is irresponsible? When does drinking alcohol change from a personal decision to a larger issue affecting society?

6. In your journal, describe what you have learned about writing while doing this unit.

7. Online Conferencing: The following activities in this unit provide good opportunities for online conferencing.

Get Set: Brainstorm online.
Live and Learn #3: Share the results of your Internet searches.
Live and Learn #5: Answer the questions online.

Unit 6 "There's a Sucker Born Every Minute"

Preparing to Write a Research Paper: Analyzing Organization

When babies are born, they like candy.

There are many people who are easily tricked or fooled into buying things.

"There's a sucker born every minute!" (P. T. Barnum) means _____

Get the Picture

Work with a group of your classmates to complete the following exercise.

A. Write three words that you would use to describe the woman in this advertisement.

1. _____   2. _____   3. _____

B. Write three words that you would use to describe the man in this advertisement.

1. _____   2. _____   3. _____

C. Write three words that you would use to describe the car.

1. _____   2. _____   3. _____

D. What product is being sold in this ad?

E. There are three idiomatic, or slang, expressions in this ad. Write them in the spaces provided.
   1.
   2.
   3.

F. Can you determine the meanings of these expressions by looking at the picture in this ad? Discuss the possible meanings with your classmates and write the meanings for each in the space provided.

1.

2.

3.

G. Think about the meaning of this ad and finish the following sentence.

If you buy a Spartan 2000, you will _____

_____

H. Do you think this advertisement tries to trick, or deceive, the consumer? If so, do you think it is successful? Why or why not?

Get Set

There are good things and bad things to be said about advertising. Use the following categories to brainstorm ideas about the pros and cons of advertising.

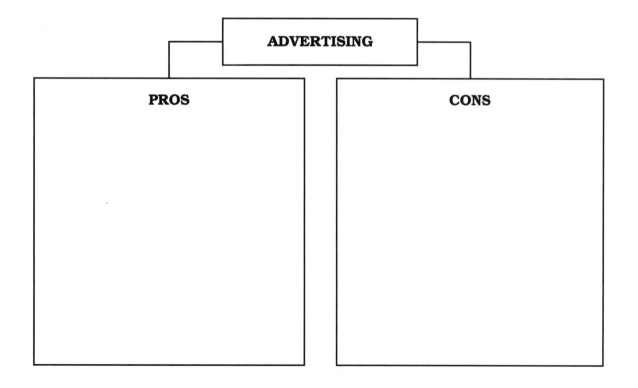

ADVERTISING	
PROS	**CONS**

Get Ready: Part 1

Understanding What You Read

As you read, it is important to try to define new words by looking at the context in which they were written. Reread the sentences that come before or after the sentence containing an unfamiliar word. Carefully read the words or phrases surrounding the new word. Often these sentences or phrases contain clues to the meaning of the new word.

Writers often help the reader by defining or explaining words they feel may be new to their audience. Following is a list of some ways writers define words in context. You may want to use this list to help you guess the meanings of new words in context.

Authors help their readers understand new vocabulary by

1. following new words with an explanation.
2. using **or** and a synonym, set off by commas, after the new word.
3. using a verb in the same or a nearby sentence that helps define the new word.
4. using an adjective or a noun in the same or a nearby sentence that helps define the new word.
5. following the new word with a set of examples.
6. providing a dictionary definition after the new word.
7. using a synonym for the new word within the same sentence or paragraph.

Read the sentences that follow and guess the meaning of the italicized vocabulary words from context. Then describe how the author has helped you make your guess.

1. An *easy sell*, a sucker, a chump—all of these terms describe people who are easily tricked or fooled into spending their money. When P. T. Barnum said, "There's a sucker born every minute," he meant that there are many such people. He also meant that business owners who understood how to *manipulate* consumers, how to convince them that they needed what the business was selling, would never have to worry about having enough business.

Definition from Context	*How the Author Helped Me*
A. easy sell—	A.
B. manipulate—	B.

2.   This idea has strongly influenced how businesses *market,* or advertise, their products.

Definition from Context	*How the Author Helped Me*
A. market—	A.

3. Critics of advertising argue that advertisers use dishonest methods in order to *deceive* the public, while supporters of advertising argue that the methods used by advertisers are fair and acceptable under the law.

Definition from Context	*How the Author Helped Me*
A. deceive—	A.

4. Every day of our lives, we are continually *bombarded* with advertising. When we turn on the radio or television, when we read a newspaper or magazine, when we walk or drive down the street we are constantly confronted with ads urging us to buy products.

Definition from Context	*How the Author Helped Me*
A. bombarded—	A.

5. Most of us do not like to think of ourselves as "suckers," but when advertisers appeal to our deepest feelings, needs, and desires, we become personally involved. Advertisers *lure* us with appealing, attractive images and language. They try to convince us that we will be better people if we use their products. Once we become convinced, they have us *hooked*. We buy because we want to be better, smarter, more attractive, and more popular.

Definition from Context	*How the Author Helped Me*
A. lure—	A.
B. hooked—	B.

6. Supporters of advertising claim that advertisers only use language and methods that are appropriate and acceptable within the limits of the law. Advertisers admit to using *exaggeration* to help sell products. Exaggeration means describing something as greater or better than it is. Advertisers exaggerate the value of products all the time by using words such as "perfect," "excellent," "natural," and "exciting." These words lead consumers to believe things that are probably not completely true, but exaggeration is an acceptable advertising *technique* that is allowed by law.

Definition from Context	*How the Author Helped Me*
A. exaggeration—	A.
B. technique—	B.

7.   Critics attack the *tactics* of advertising, especially advertising targeted at children
and teenagers. They say advertisers use images that are especially appealing to
youth. They use cartoons, games, and prizes to attract young consumers who are
not yet capable of being critical consumers.

Definition from Context	*How the Author Helped Me*
A. tactics—	A.

Get Ready: Part 2

Share your guesses with the rest of the class and discuss the different ways the author helped the reader understand the vocabulary through context. How did you know what each word meant?

Go for It

You defined words from context in the last exercise. Now, read the composition "Are You an Easy Sell?" Use the reading strategies you have learned to help you understand any other new words that may be confusing to you.

Are You an Easy Sell?

An easy sell, a sucker, a chump—all of these terms describe people who are easily tricked or fooled into spending their money. When P. T. Barnum said, "There's a sucker born every minute," he meant that there are many such people. He also meant that business owners who understood how to manipulate consumers, how to convince them that they needed what the business was selling, would never have to worry about having enough business. This idea has strongly influenced how businesses market, or advertise, their products. Critics of advertising say that advertisers use dishonest methods to deceive the public while supporters of advertising argue that the methods used by advertisers are fair and acceptable under the law.

Every day of our lives, we are continually bombarded with advertising. When we turn on the radio or television, when we read a newspaper or magazine, when we walk or drive down the street we are constantly confronted with ads urging us to buy products. Even if we don't want to pay attention to ads, we can't get away from them. They are in our mailboxes, on the Internet, at the movies, and on every product that we buy. In his book *Doublespeak,* William Lutz states that "the first rule of advertising is that nothing is what it seems. . . ." If that's true, we need to be aware that advertisers may be trying to play us for suckers.

Most of us do not like to think of ourselves as "suckers," but when advertisers appeal to our deepest feelings, needs, and desires, we become personally involved. Advertisers lure us with appealing, attractive images and language. They try to convince us that we will be better people if we use their products. Once we become convinced, they have us hooked. We buy because we want to be better, smarter, more attractive, and more popular.

Critics of advertising argue that advertisers use dishonest methods in order to deceive the public. They say advertisers trick consumers by using language that is confusing. For example, some advertisements sent through the mail suggest that the reader "may already be a winner" of an 11 million dollar sweepstakes contest. Other ads hook consumers by announcing in large print that consumers can get something for free, but when they read the small print, they find out that they must purchase something else first. Critics say that advertisers use "doublespeak" to communicate their message. "Doublespeak" is language that appears to communicate the truth but actually expresses lies. "Doublespeak" occurs when words like *better* and *best* are used to describe a product, but there is no basis in fact to make such a judgment.

Supporters of advertising claim that advertisers only use language and methods that are appropriate and acceptable within the limits of the law. Advertisers admit to using exaggeration to help sell products. Exaggeration means describing something as greater or better than it is. Advertisers exaggerate the value of products all the time by using words such as "perfect," "excellent," "natural," and "exciting." These words lead consumers to believe things that are probably not completely true, but exaggeration is an acceptable advertising technique that is allowed by law.

Critics attack the tactics of advertising, especially advertising targeted at children and teenagers. They say advertisers use images that are especially appealing to youth. They use cartoons, games, and prizes to attract young consumers who are not yet capable of being critical buyers. As an example, critics point out that carefully planned advertising campaigns by tobacco companies have resulted in hooking youth on nicotine.

Advertisers openly acknowledge that they use different types of appeals to market their products. Sex, humor, testimony, and reward appeals are just a few of their marketing techniques. They insist, however, that using tricks and gimmicks to sell products is as old as the advertising business itself, and they point out that exaggerating the value of a product and offering prizes are legal.

Advertisers insist that they provide a vital service to consumers. After all, every day millions of consumers must make decisions about spending their hard-earned money. How will they spend their money, and on what will they base their decisions? Supporters see advertising as a way to inform consumers. Critics accuse advertisers of only being concerned with selling more products and making more money even if it means deceiving people to do so. In the end, it is up to each individual to become a critical and informed consumer; otherwise we are all just suckers, fools easily parted from our money.

Give-and-Take

Work with a partner or in small groups to make a list of the main points from the article.

Get Real

Looking at the Parts of a Composition

Read the following information, answer the questions, and share your answers with the class.

A. Title

Choosing a good title for a composition is important. You don't want a title that is too broad or too general. A good title arouses the reader's interest and introduces the topic. It often indicates the direction the writing will take. For example, it can indicate whether the tone will be light or serious.

Look back at the composition in this unit. What is the title of the composition?

Does the title indicate to you what the topic of the composition is? How?

Did the title make you want to read the article? Why or why not?

Do you think the title is a good title? Why or why not?

What title might you give to this composition?

B. Topic Sentence

You have already learned that every paragraph has a topic sentence. The topic sentence is supported, or developed, by the rest of the sentences in the paragraph.

C. Parts of a Composition

A complete composition consists of a series of paragraphs. In a standard composition these paragraphs are organized into three parts. The first part is called the **introduction.**

Can you name the other two parts?

1. <u>Introduction</u>   2. _____   3. _____

1. Introduction

   In your previous writings you have included a sentence that tells the main idea of the whole composition.

   In your own words, what is the main idea of "Are You an Easy Sell?"

   The sentence that states the main idea of the whole composition is called the **thesis statement.** The thesis statement is stated within the introduction of a composition. All of the paragraphs in a composition develop or prove the main idea of the whole composition.

   The thesis statement for the composition "Are You an Easy Sell?" is found in the introduction, in the first paragraph. Reread the first paragraph and find the thesis statement, the sentence that states the central idea of the whole article. Write the thesis statement here.

   _____

   _____

   _____

   The introduction of a composition can be more than one paragraph long, and the thesis statement can be stated anywhere in the introduction.

   How many paragraphs are in the introduction of this composition?

   An effective introduction immediately grabs the attention of the reader and then prepares the reader for what will follow in the body of the composition. There are many ways that writers introduce a composition. Sometimes writers will

   - tell a narrative story that directly relates to the topic of the composition
   - pose a question
   - open with a quote
   - begin with a definition
   - remind the readers of a recent or well-known event
   - grab the audience with startling statistics or facts
   - state a strong or controversial opinion.

How does the introduction of this composition grab the reader's attention?

How does the introduction prepare the reader for what will follow in the body of the paper?

2. The Body
The paragraphs that follow the introduction are called the **body.** In the body of the composition, the writer develops or proves the central idea stated in the thesis statement. The writer provides supporting paragraphs that develop or prove the central idea. These paragraphs include subtopics and support in the form of examples, reasons, explanations, facts, definitions, statistics, and causes and consequences.

Reread the body of this composition.

How many paragraphs make up the body of the composition?

Underline the topic sentence of each one.

Do the supporting sentences support each topic sentence?

Does the information in each of these paragraphs prove or develop the thesis statement? How?

If not, which ones are off topic?

3. The Conclusion

There are many different ways to conclude a composition. One of the most common is to *restate the thesis and to summarize the most important points* in the composition. Or writers might choose to

- tell a closing story directly related to the issue
- refer back to the introduction
- repeat the problem and challenge the readers to become involved
- ask the readers a question
- offer solutions to the problem.

Or writers may do more than one of these.

Read the conclusion of this composition.

Does it follow the most common pattern for concluding a composition?

If not, what pattern does it follow?

Does this conclusion support the thesis statement? Why or why not?

Work It Out

1. In the body and conclusion of "Are You an Easy Sell?" the author presents two different points of view about the issue of manipulating consumers through advertising, the perspective of supporters of advertising and the perspective of critics of advertising.

   a. Go back to the reading and number the paragraphs.
   b. Use the tree diagram that follows to help you see how the author has organized the paper. Identify in which paragraph each subtopic and viewpoint are covered and write the number of the paragraph in the appropriate box in the tree diagram. The first one has been done for you. It indicates that the critics' viewpoint about language used in advertising is covered in paragraph 4.

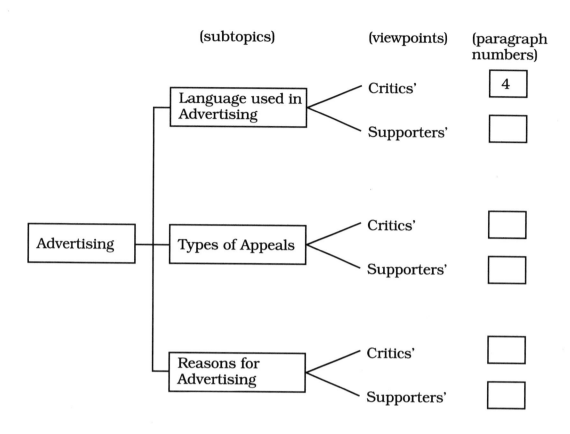

2. Is there a pattern as to how the author presents both points of view? If so, what is it? What is another pattern the author might use to organize this paper?

3. What kinds of support does the author give for critics' and supporters' views? Check all that apply.

__ definitions
__ examples
__ explanations
__ details
__ reasons
__ facts
__ statistics
__ other (identify)_____

4. Is the author a supporter or a critic of advertising, or is the author neutral? How do you know?

5. What was the author's purpose in writing this paper?

6. Who was the intended audience? How do you know?

7. Are you a supporter or a critic of advertising methods? Why?

Pull It Together

So far in this unit,

- you have thought about and discussed an advertisement with your classmates;
- you have defined new vocabulary through context and have seen how writers consider and write for their audience when using words that may be unfamiliar to their readers;
- you have listed some of the pros and cons of advertising;
- you have identified and analyzed the three main parts of a standard composition;
- you have identified the thesis statement of a composition;
- you have analyzed the organization and content of a composition and considered purpose, audience, and perspective, or viewpoint.

Now, write about one of the following controversial issues or come up with an issue of your own. You must write so that your audience can identify both sides of the issue. Your classmates will be your audience. You don't know what they may know about the issue or how they feel about it. Consider your audience and be prepared to define or explain terms in context. After you have chosen a topic, read through the steps outlined in the next activity, Get Going. They will help you organize your paper.

Some controversial issues

Should smoking be allowed in public buildings?

Should alcohol be allowed on college campuses?

Should women receive equal pay for equal work?

Should music lyrics be rated for content the same way that movies are rated?

Should women be allowed to fight in combat beside men?

Should alcohol and tobacco advertisements be allowed on billboards?

Should campus dormitories be coed?

Get Going: Part 1

Use these steps if you need help in organizing your paper.

1. Brainstorm ideas about the topic you have chosen. Use one or more of the methods you have learned so far.

    - draw a cluster diagram
    - make a list of your ideas
    - make a tree diagram
    - freewrite
    - make a chart similar to the chart in Get Set
    - talk about your topic with a friend or classmate

2. Review your ideas and decide how you want to focus your paper. Then write your thesis statement.

3. Review your list of ideas and choose the ones that best support your thesis statement. (Omit those that don't support your thesis statement.) Divide these ideas into subtopics (the topics for each paragraph). Some of your ideas will become subtopics, and some will become support. You may want to make an outline or a chart to help you organize your paper.

Get Going: Part 2

1. Use your subtopics to help you write a topic sentence for each paragraph.
2. Write supporting sentences for each topic sentence. Remember that supporting sentences can include examples, definitions, explanations, details, facts, reasons, and statistics.
3. Put your subtopics and support into a logical order.
4. Remember to consider your audience.
5. If you have trouble writing your introduction or conclusion or giving your composition a title, refer back to Get Real for ideas.

After you have finished your draft, give it to a classmate to read.

Just Do It

Read your classmate's paper. Then answer the following questions in your classmate's book and make a tree diagram of your classmate's paper.

1. How many paragraphs are in the introduction?

2. What is the main idea of your classmate's paper?

3. Find the thesis statement in your classmate's paper and underline it.
4. On a separate piece of paper, make a tree diagram of your classmate's paper, similar to the one used in Work It Out. Start by identifying the topic and the subtopics. Then identify in which paragraph critics' and supporters' viewpoints about each subtopic are stated.

5. What kinds of support does your classmate give for critics' and supporters' views? Check all that apply.

    __ definitions
    __ examples
    __ explanations
    __ details
    __ reasons
    __ facts
    __ statistics
    __ other (identify)_____

After you have finished answering the questions and have made a tree diagram of your classmate's paper, give your answers, the diagram, and your classmate's composition back to your classmate. Then revise your own composition as needed.

Now give this draft to your teacher. Your teacher will use the following form, Fix It Up, to help you further revise your paper.

Fix It Up

Student's Name _____

Check the boxes that apply.

1. The title arouses interest and tells the reader what the paper is about.

   __ yes   __ no

2. The introduction catches the reader's interest.

   __ yes   __ no

3. The thesis statement is clearly stated in the introduction.

   __ yes   __ no

4. The thesis statement adequately expresses the main idea.

   __ yes   __ no

5. Each paragraph supports or develops the main idea of the paper.

   __ yes   __ no

6. Each paragraph has a topic sentence.

   __ yes   __ no

7. The supporting points are clearly stated.

   __ yes   __ no

   __ They need to be explained more fully.

   __ They contain enough details, examples, and concrete evidence.

   __ Some should be eliminated.

   __ All of the examples are relevant.

8. The points are presented in a logical and useful order.

   __ yes   __ no

   You might want to move the following information.

9. The draft contains a strong conclusion that supports the paper.

   __ yes   __ no

Polish It

Read your teacher's comments in Fix It Up and make all of the necessary changes.
When you have finished revising your paper, go to Polish It in the Appendix at the
back of this book. Use the editing checklist to help you look for grammatical and
mechanical problems in your paper.

Evaluate Yourself   Name _____

Reread your paper and fill in the following form.

1. Check all that apply.
    The title of my paper

    ___ a. arouses interest.
    ___ b. introduces the topic.
    ___ c. indicates the direction the writing will take.

2. My paper includes an introduction, a body, and a conclusion.
    ___ yes   ___ no

3. In the introduction, I grab the attention of the reader and prepare the reader by

    _____

    _____

4. The thesis statement is included in the introduction.
    ___ yes   ___ no

5. My thesis statement is _____

6. My thesis statement describes the main idea of the paper.
    ___ yes   ___ no

7. In the body of the composition, I develop or prove the main idea stated in my the-
    sis statement by stating reasons, defining terms, providing examples, or using
    other kinds of support.
    ___ yes   ___ no

8. All of my paragraphs have topic sentences and supporting sentences.
    ___ yes   ___ no

9. My supporting sentences have enough details, examples, and concrete evidence to
    support the topic sentences.
    ___ yes   ___ no

10. My paper presents both points of view.
    __ yes   __ no

11. I conclude the composition by _____

    _____

12. I'm having trouble with

Using your answers on this form as a guide, revise your paper by making any changes you wish to make to it. Now give the final draft of your paper and this self-evaluation to your teacher.

Teacher Feedback

Student's Name _____

Structure

1. Your paper includes an introduction, a body, and a conclusion.
   __ yes   __ no

2. Your paper includes a thesis statement that tells the main idea of the whole paper. Your thesis statement is:

3. Your thesis statement is in the introduction of your paper.
   __ yes   __ no

4. Check one.

   __ a. Your paper presents the information in a logical order.
   __ b. Your paper does not present the information in a logical order.

   _____

   _____

5. One grammar structure that you seem to be having difficulty with is

Content

1. Check all that apply.
   The title of your composition

   __ a. arouses interest.
   __ b. introduces the topic.
   __ c. indicates the direction the writing will take.

2. Check all that apply.

    The introduction of your composition grabs my interest and prepares me for what will follow by

    __ a. telling a narrative story that relates to the topic.
    __ b. posing a question.
    __ c. opening with a quote.
    __ d. opening with a definition.
    __ e. bringing up a recent or well-known event.
    __ f. presenting startling statistics or facts.
    __ g. stating a strong or controversial opinion.
    __ h. other: _____

3. All of the paragraphs in your composition relate directly to the thesis statement.
    __ yes   __ no

    Paragraph(s) # _____ do(es) not relate directly to your thesis statement.
4. All of your paragraphs have topic sentences.
    __ yes   __ no

    Paragraph(s) # _____ do(es) not have topic sentences.
5. You present enough details, examples, and concrete evidence to support your topic sentences.
    __ yes   __ no

    Paragraph(s) # _____ need(s) more support.
6. You have presented both points of view.
    __ yes   __ no
7. Check all that apply.

    In the conclusion of your composition

    __ a. you restate and summarize the most important points in the composition.
    __ b. you tell a closing story related to the issue.
    __ c. you refer back to the introduction.
    __ d. you repeat the problem and challenge the readers to become involved.
    __ e. you ask the readers a question.
    __ f. you offer solutions to the problem.
    __ g. other: _____

8. What I find most interesting about your paper is

9. What I'd like to know more about is

10. Other comments

Live and Learn

Additional Activities and Journal Assignments

1. Choose one of the issues listed in Pull It Together that is different from the one you wrote about. In your journal, write about this new issue from the viewpoints of a supporter and of a critic.

2. Invent a new product. Draw a picture of it. Describe its use. Now come up with an advertising campaign for your product. How will you advertise? What will you say in your ads? Who will you target? You may use exaggeration in your ads, but you may not use doublespeak. (See the reading "Are You an Easy Sell?" in this unit for the definition of doublespeak.) Write down your ideas. Share them with your class-mates.

3. Invite a graphic artist who works in advertising to visit your class to speak about his or her work. Ask about the purpose of advertising and about the language and the techniques used in advertising.

4. Find two ads that feature the same kind of product (e.g., two different brands of soft drinks). In what way do these ads appeal to consumers? Do they try to deceive the consumer? Are they successful? Is one ad more effective than the other? Write your responses to these questions and any other comments you have about the ads in your journal.

5. Read some articles from newspapers or magazines. Look at the title of each one. Do the titles arouse interest? Do they indicate the direction the articles will take? Look at the introduction of each. How do the introductions grab the attention of the reader and prepare the reader for what will follow? Look at the conclusion of each article. How is each conclusion developed?

6. In your journal, describe what you have learned about writing while doing this unit.

7. Online Conferencing: The following activities in this unit provide good opportunities for online conferencing.

   Get Set: Brainstorm online.
   Live and Learn #1: Teachers: post one of the controversial issues from Pull It Together online. Students: your teacher has posted a controversial issue online. Read the issue and decide whether you are a supporter or a critic. Post your position. Then read your classmates' positions and respond.

Unit 7   Tell It Like It Is

Preparing to Write
a Research Paper:
Quoting and Paraphrasing

Tell it like it is means_____

Get the Picture

Write answers to the following questions. Share your answers with your classmates.

1. What is the man asking the woman?

2. Why does she answer him the way she does?

3. What issue is being raised in this picture?

4. Does this public service ad *tell it like it is?*

Get Real

A. We often use quotations as a way to tell it like it is. When writing papers we may use quotations from different sources to support the main ideas. Brainstorm answers to the following question with your class.

    What guidelines should you follow when you want to include quotations in your papers?

B. Complete each sentence on the left by choosing the correct ending from the choices given on the right. Write the letter(s) of the correct choice next to the number in the blanks provided.

1. __ A quotation . . .

    A. when you want to use the exact words from the original source. This is often true when you want to quote statistics.

2. __ When you write a paper, it is important to express your ideas . . .

    B. your paper to become a collection of quotations.

3. __ You do not want . . .

    C. uses the exact words of your original source and is marked by quotation marks (") at the beginning and end of the sentence(s).

4. __, __, __ You should only use quotations . . .

    D. when the person being quoted is an authority on the subject.

    E. in your own words.

    F. when the language has great emotional, historical, or metaphorical appeal.

C. Choose one of the sentences from this matching exercise and quote it directly here. Be sure to use appropriate punctuation.

_____

_____

D. Did the guidelines that you came up with for using quotations include the same information as the matching exercise? If not, add the missing information to your list.

Get Ready

When you put someone else's ideas into your own words, you are paraphrasing. Paraphrasing shows that you truly understand someone else's ideas, and it also shows how proficient you are in English. Paraphrasing is similar to summarizing except that when you paraphrase, you are usually working with short passages consisting of a few sentences and sometimes only one sentence.

A. There are two initial steps to writing a good paraphrase.
    1. Read a passage and be certain that you understand it.
    2. Without looking back at the passage, write the passage using your own words.
        Compare your passage with the original to see if your passage means the same
        thing and to be sure that your passage uses different vocabulary and sentence
        structure. If the original passage contains technical vocabulary that does not
        have an equivalent, it is permissible to use such vocabulary without using
        quotation marks.

Smoking has been prohibited in many
shopping malls, restaurants, and other
public places. New regulations about
smoking are being implemented throughout
the United States.

Read the caption beside the graphic. Now, read the following paraphrases and
put a check mark by the one that best expresses the meaning of the original
passage.

__ New laws about smoking are taking effect across the country. Smoking has
    been banned in places where people shop, eat, and congregate.
__ Many places frequented by the populace such as shopping centers and
    eateries have severely restricted smoking. All around the country, smoking
    codes of conduct are being imposed.

Does this paraphrase mean the same thing as the original without repeating the vocabulary or sentence structure?

Now write your own paraphrase for the caption.

3. If the paraphrase you have written contains too many words from the original, you will need to add a third step. The third step requires you to use a thesaurus and/or a dictionary to help you replace key words or phrases from the original passage. This can be dangerous if you simply replace key words without changing how the ideas are expressed. An acceptable paraphrase means the same thing as the original without repeating the vocabulary or sentence structure.

B. Read the following passage.

Smokers complain that many of these policies are unfair. In an article entitled "The Latest on Office Smoking Bans" by Eugenie Allen, published in *Glamour,* one secretary complained that while secretaries and junior executives cannot smoke at their desks, higher-level executives have no such restriction.

1. Paraphrase the passage using the first two steps (i.e., read and understand the passage; then write what it means in your own words). Then compare your paraphrase with the original. If it contains too many of the same words as the original, you will need to complete the third step.
2. Exchange your paraphrase with a classmate. Does your classmate's paraphrase mean the same thing as the original without repeating the vocabulary or sentence structure?
3. If your paraphrase contained too many words from the original, make a list of those words and find synonyms for them using a dictionary and/or thesaurus to help you. For example:

Original	*Synonym*
secretaries	office workers
lawyers	attorneys

4. Now, think about what the passage means and write your paraphrase using the synonyms you have found.

_____

_____

_____

_____

Work It Out

A. The following paragraphs appear in an article entitled "Smokers Left out in the Cold." Passages in the paragraphs have been numbered. First read the paragraphs. Then decide which passages would be appropriate as quotations, which passages would be appropriate as paraphrases, and which information you would choose to omit if you were doing research for a paper about bans on office smoking. Don't paraphrase every passage. The passages you choose to paraphrase should show that you understand the most important points in a reading.

(1) Environmental tobacco smoke (ETS), also known as passive smoke or secondhand smoke, causes lung cancer in healthy nonsmokers. Passive smoking occurs when nonsmokers breathe in tobacco smoke from smokers' cigarettes. **(2)** The U.S. Environmental Protection Agency (EPA) issued a report in 1992 that stated that 3,000 nonsmokers die annually from lung cancer caused by ETS. **(3)** This smoking statistic has fueled a new debate.

(4) Since that report came out, employers in both the public and private sectors have been concerned about possible lawsuits by nonsmoking employees claiming their lung cancer was caused by secondhand smoke at the workplace. **(5)** This concern has led to restrictions on smoking in many public workplaces. Following the EPA report, California passed a law forbidding smoking in all buildings owned or leased by the state. Forty-eight other states and the District of Columbia now limit or prohibit smoking in public places. Many federal work sites are completely smoke free, including the White House.

(6) Federal laws governing smoking have been passed that affect smoking in the private sector as well. **(7)** Congress banned smoking on all domestic airplane flights of six hours or less. Many flight attendants breathe a sigh of relief at not having to inhale passengers' cigarette smoke. As one attendant said, "I couldn't stand it. The smoke bothered my eyes, gave me headaches, and made me feel nauseous. It was hard to work under those conditions."

B. Now, decide which passages you would quote directly, which passages you would paraphrase, and which information you would not include in a research paper about smoking bans. Write the number of each passage under the appropriate category in the boxes. Remember as you are choosing passages to quote or paraphrase, choose only those that state main points.

Quotations	Paraphrases	Omit

Now discuss your choices with the class.

C. Choose two of the passages that would be appropriate for paraphrasing in a research paper. Follow the steps previously described and write a paraphrase for each of those two passages in the space provided.

1. Paraphrase of passage # _____

_____

_____

2. Paraphrase of passage # _____

_____

_____

D. Now, exchange paraphrases with a classmate. Do your classmate's paraphrases mean the same thing as the originals without repeating the vocabulary or sentence structure?

Go for It

You have already paraphrased three paragraphs from the article "Smokers Left out in the Cold." Now, read the entire article.

Smokers Left out in the Cold

"Frankly, I'd consider suing the college I work for if I got lung cancer. I don't smoke, but two of my coworkers at nearby desks do. I've told my supervisor, but since she smokes too, she's not too concerned about the problem," claimed a college secretary.

Environmental tobacco smoke (ETS), also known as passive smoke or secondhand smoke, causes lung cancer in healthy nonsmokers. Passive smoking occurs when nonsmokers breathe in tobacco smoke from smokers' cigarettes. The U.S. Environmental Protection Agency (EPA) issued a report in 1992 that stated that 3,000 nonsmokers die annually from lung cancer caused by ETS. This smoking statistic has fueled a new debate.

Since that report came out, employers in both the public and private sectors have been concerned about possible lawsuits by nonsmoking employees claiming their lung cancer was caused by secondhand smoke at the workplace. This concern has led to restrictions on smoking in many public workplaces. Following the EPA report, California passed a law forbidding smoking in all buildings owned or leased by the state. Forty-eight other states and the District of Columbia now limit or prohibit smoking in public places. Many federal work sites are completely smoke free, including the White House.

Federal laws governing smoking have been passed that affect smoking in the private sector as well. Congress banned smoking on all domestic airplane flights of six hours or less. Many flight attendants breathe a sigh of relief at not having to inhale passengers' cigarette smoke. As one attendant said, "I couldn't stand it. The smoke bothered my eyes, gave me headaches, and made me feel nauseous. It was hard to work under those conditions."

Many private companies have also enacted "no smoking" policies to avoid possible litigation in the future. Approximately one-third of American businesses have "no smoking" regulations, and another third prohibit smoking in open offices. Smokers complain that many of these policies are unfair. In an article entitled "The Latest on Office Smoking

Bans" by Eugenie Allen, published in *Glamour,* one secretary complained that while sec-retaries and junior executives cannot smoke at their desks, higher-level executives have no such restriction. They can smoke in their private offices. "It's not fair," agrees another administrative assistant. "We have to stand outside to smoke while the higher-ups can enjoy a cigarette without leaving the comfort of their offices."

Smokers may be tired of having to stand outside to smoke, but nonsmokers continue to complain of the health risks associated with ETS. The issue is heated and causes a great deal of tension between smokers and nonsmokers. However, despite the ongoing debate among coworkers, employers prefer not to risk costly lawsuits. They are coming down hard on smoking in the workplace, leaving smokers out in the cold.

Get Going 　　　　Name _____

A. With your class, discuss the main idea of the article. Then find the thesis statement and underline it.

B. Choose two additional passages from the article to paraphrase. Remember to choose passages that state a main point. Write the passages and your paraphrases in the space provided.

Passage: _____

_____

_____

Paraphrase: _____

_____

_____

Passage: _____

_____

_____

Paraphrase: _____

_____

_____

C. Hand in your paraphrases to your teacher.

Pull It Together

So far in this unit,

- you have learned the guidelines for using quotations and have practiced selecting the best passages to quote;
- you have learned a two-step approach to writing paraphrases and have practiced writing paraphrases;
- you have learned how a thesaurus and a dictionary can help you with paraphrasing;
- you have practiced choosing passages that express the most important points;
- you have read a short article, isolated important passages, and paraphrased those passages.

Now, do the following.

1. Find a one- to two-page article about a health issue. You can find short articles in popular magazines (such as *Health, Time, Newsweek, Prevention, Glamour,* or *Mother Jones*), in journals (such as *Current Health 2*), on the Internet (in locations such as *Youth Partnership for Health*), in health-related pamphlets available at student health centers, county health agencies, and doctors' offices.
2. Read the article and choose one passage to quote and two passages to paraphrase. Remember, paraphrasing is similar to summarizing in that you must restate the ideas in your own words.
3. Write the original passages, your paraphrases, and the quotation on a separate sheet of paper.
4. Number your paraphrases.

   After you have finished writing your paraphrases and quote, give a copy of the original article and your quote and paraphrases to a classmate to check. Your classmate will

   a. check the quotation and each paraphrase to see whether you have chosen passages that highlight main points from the article
   b. look carefully at your quotation to be sure that you have used the exact words from the original passages and have included appropriate punctuation
   c. check your paraphrases to see if they mean the same thing as the originals without repeating the vocabulary or sentence structure.

Just Do It

Read your classmate's article. Then, use the following checklist in your classmate's book to evaluate your classmate's paraphrases and quotations.

1. My classmate chose only important points to quote and paraphrase.
   __ yes   __ no
2. The quotation provides information that

   __ contains statistics
   __ comes from an authority
   __ has language with great emotional, historical, or metaphorical appeal.

3. The quotation repeats the exact words from the original and is punctuated correctly.
   __ yes   __ no
4. Paraphrase #1 means the same thing as the original.
   __ yes   __ no

   Paraphrase #2 means the same thing as the original.
   __ yes   __ no
5. Paraphrase #1 changes the key words and expressions from the original.
   __ yes   __ no

   Paraphrase # 2 changes the key words and expressions from the original.
   __ yes   __ no
6. Paraphrase #1 changes the sentence structure from the original.
   __ yes   __ no

   Paraphrase #2 changes the sentence structure from the original.
   __ yes   __ no

When you have finished, give the article, your classmate's paraphrases and quote, and this checklist to your classmate. Make any changes you want to make to your own quote and paraphrases at this time.

Evaluate Yourself

Name _____

Reread your paraphrases and quotation and fill in the following form.

1. I have shown that I understand the most important points in the article by the passages that I have chosen to paraphrase and quote.
   __ yes   __ no

2. The quotation repeats the exact words from the original and is punctuated correctly.
   __ yes   __ no

3. My paraphrases express the same meaning as the original passages without repeating key words and expressions
   __ yes   __ no

4. My paraphrases express the ideas of the original without using the same sentence structure.
   __ yes   __ no

5. I'm having trouble with

Now give your quotation and paraphrases, your original article, and this self-evaluation to your teacher.

Teacher Feedback   Student's Name _____

1. Your choice of passages shows that you understood the most important points in the reading.

   __ yes   __ no

   If not, you need to omit the following passages that don't include important information and replace them with passages that do state important information.

2. The quotation provides information that
   __ contains statistics
   __ comes from an authority
   __ has language with great emotional, historical, or metaphorical appeal.

3. The quotation repeats the exact words from the original and is punctuated correctly.

   __ yes   __ no

4. Paraphrase #1 has the same meaning as the original.

   __ yes   __ no

   Paraphrase #2 has the same meaning as the original.

   __ yes   __ no

5. Paraphrase #1 changes the key words and expressions from original.

   __ yes   __ no

   Paraphrase #2 changes the key words and expressions from the original.

   __ yes   __ no

6. Paraphrase #1 changes key words and expressions, but the sentence structure is too close to the original.

   __ yes   __ no

   Paraphrase #2 changes key words and expressions, but the sentence structure is too close to the original.

   __ yes   __ no

7. You clearly understand the guidelines for paraphrasing and quoting.

   __ yes   __ no

   You need additional work on paraphrasing and quoting.

   __ yes   __ no

8. Other comments

Live and Learn

Additional Activities and Journal Assignments

1. Read another short article about a topic of interest to you. Choose two passages to paraphrase and one to quote. Remember to choose only passages that state important points. Show your quote and paraphrases to a classmate or your teacher for feedback.

2. Analyze the organization of the article "Smokers Left out in the Cold." Make an outline or a chart for the article. What is the topic of each paragraph? What kind of information supports the topic in each paragraph? Do all of the paragraphs support the thesis statement? How many paragraphs are in the introduction? How does the introduction grab the interest of the reader? How does the author conclude the paper?

3. Does the article "Smokers Left out in the Cold" present more than one point of view? Is the author neutral? How do you know? What was the author's purpose in writing this paper? Who was the intended audience? How do you know? Write answers to these questions in your journal.

4. Think about the title of the article "Smokers Left out in the Cold." Does the title arouse interest, introduce the topic, or indicate the direction the writing will take? What title would you give this article? Write about this in your journal.

5. Analyze the content and organization of the article you used in Pull It Together. Use questions 1 through 3 in Live and Learn as a guide.

6. What do you think about smoking? Should smokers be allowed to smoke in public buildings such as restaurants and malls? Should smokers be allowed to smoke in taverns and pubs? What rights should smokers have? What rights should non-smokers have? Write your thoughts about these questions in your journal.

7. In your journal, describe what you have learned about writing while doing this unit.

8. Online Conferencing: The following activities in this unit provide good opportunities for online conferencing.

    Get the Picture: Answer the questions about the picture online.
    Get Ready, B: Share paraphrases online. Evaluate your classmates' paraphrases and offer suggestions.
    Live and Learn #6: Discuss this issue online.

Unit 8   Wrap It Up

Writing a Research Paper

Go wrap a gift.

Finish the task.

Wrap it up means _____

Get the Picture

1. These three pictures represent a three-step approach to writing a research paper. Work with a partner to find words or phrases that describe this approach. Write your words or phrases under the pictures.
2. Discuss these three steps with your whole class.

In this unit, you will practice ways to prepare for writing a short research paper. You will inquire about, investigate, and research an issue related to health. Then, you will write a short research paper.

Get Set

Inquire: Part 1

A. Work with your class to brainstorm topics about health. Use the cluster diagram on this page as a guide. You may need to add more bubbles to the diagram.

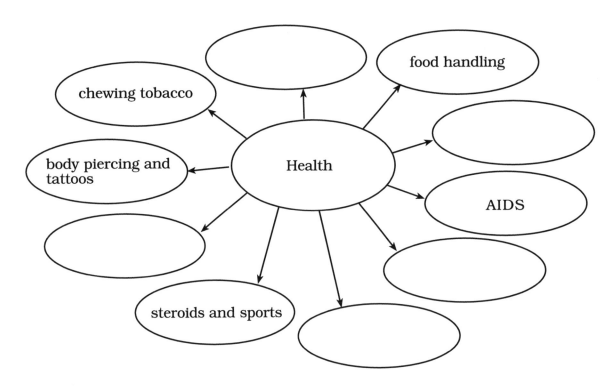

B. Ask yourself which one of these topics you already know something about or which one you want to find out about. Choose one topic and spend 10 minutes writing about it on a separate sheet of paper. Connect ideas about the topic to your own thoughts and experiences. Try to write without stopping. Keep this freewrite exercise and use it as you explore your topic further.

Inquire: Part 2

A. Write your topic on a piece of paper. Now pass your paper to each of your classmates. Your classmates will write on your paper what they know about your topic or a question they may have about your topic. You will do the same for your classmates. Collect your classmates' ideas and questions about your topic and use them as you explore your topic further.

B. Write down at least six questions you would like to have answered about your topic.

Inquire: Part 3

A. Look at the information and questions you have gathered from your freewrite exercise, your classmates, and your own questions. Choose one to explore for a research paper. Then narrow your topic by writing exploratory sentences. For example, if you decided to explore the topic of smoking, you may have found the sentence "Smoking is bad for your health" among the information you gathered. Your exploratory sentences might read as follows.

I already know that smoking is bad for a smoker's health.
I want to find out the facts about *how* smoking is harmful, what the physical effects of smoking are.

Write your own exploratory sentences on the lines provided.

I already know _____

I want to know _____

B. Now, try to focus or limit your topic by writing the main question that you want to explore in your research paper. Using our example for a paper about smoking, the main question becomes

What are the effects of smoking on the human body?

Think about the exploratory sentences you wrote. What question do you want to explore in your research paper? Write your main question here.

C. The main question leads to a focused topic. For the main question, *What are the effects of smoking on the human body?* the focused topic becomes

The Effects of Smoking on the Human Body

Change your main question into a focused topic. Write your focused topic here.

D. Now that you have limited your topic, you should find it easy to write a preliminary thesis statement. The first thesis statement you write is called preliminary because your statement may change as you discover new information during your research. Even though your thesis statement may change, your preliminary thesis is necessary to help you organize your paper. Remember, your paper must support or prove your thesis statement.

A preliminary thesis statement for the effects of smoking on the human body might be

Smoking harms the body in many ways.

Think about your focused topic and write your preliminary thesis statement here.

Get Ready: Part 1

Investigate

A. Work with a group of your classmates to brainstorm places you might find additional information about your topics. Divide your list into *Library Sources* and *Other Sources*. Share your list with the class.

Library Sources	*Other Sources*
1. current newspaper articles	1. surveys
2.	2.
3.	3.
4.	4.
5.	5.

B. Some of these sources would be more useful than others for writing a short research paper. Think about your topic and put a check mark by the ones you think would be most useful to you.

C. You may be familiar with finding and using the sources you listed that are outside of the library but unfamiliar with how to find and use sources within a library. Being able to use the sources in a library is key to successful research. You may need to ask your teacher to do a lesson on finding and using sources in libraries, or you may need to visit your local library and request assistance from the librarians. Don't be shy about asking for help in a library. It is part of a librarian's job to guide people through the search process.

D. Work with your classmates to fill in the missing information.
   As you locate your sources, you will need to keep records. You need to write down

1. the full titles of books, magazines or journals, and articles

2.

3.

4.

5. the name of the publisher and the city of publication of each book.

E. Choose either a or b and complete each of the following sentences on the lines provided.

      a. you can simply record the information in a notebook for later use.
      b. you should use note cards to record the information from your sources.

1. In a long research paper, which usually requires more than five references,

_____

_____

2. However, in a short research paper, which usually requires fewer than five

references, _____

_____

Get Ready: Part 2

As you find your sources, you need to skim each one to determine whether it contains information that supports your preliminary thesis statement. Often you will find that the information from your sources can be sorted into categories. For example, information about the effects of smoking on the human body could be sorted into the following categories.

Problem	Causes	Consequences	Reasons	Solutions

A. There are many different ways to sort information. Some possible ways are listed here. Discuss them with your class and add to the list. Then with your class, answer the questions that follow.

- state problems, facts, or myths about a topic
- cover causes, reasons, benefits, consequences
- propose solutions or preventive measures
- contrast the pros and cons or the similarities and differences
- review the past and present and project into the future
- predict effects or outcomes

In what ways do categories help writers?

Why do writers include more than one category in the same article?

B. With your class, brainstorm logical categories for the following topics.

1. Advertising during the 1990s
2. Alcohol use on college campuses
3. Cultural differences between Americans and Canadians
4. The Effects of dance on physical and mental health
5. What rap music means to teenagers

Don't Be a Copycat

A. When you start to read from the sources that you find, you will notice that some information is common to most or all of the sources. This information consists of well-known facts among those who have studied the topic. It is this information that you will summarize in your own words, and it will make up the bulk of your paper.

But you will also want to identify passages that are unique to one source. These you will want to quote or paraphrase for use as support in your research paper. Copy these special sentences and passages into a notebook. This step is important because you may not have time to reread entire articles as you write your paper and you will need to find passages quickly.

B.   Whether you quote or paraphrase someone else's ideas in your paper, you must give credit to the author whose ideas or words you are using. It is considered plagiarism not to do so. Plagiarism is stealing someone else's words and/or ideas and can have serious consequences.

In a short research paper, you give credit to the author by using parenthetical citations. Citations give credit to the source of your information. There are different styles for citing sources within a paper. For your purposes, you are going to use the author-date system. This system is favored in the social sciences, biology, earth sciences, and business. The following examples show the style for using parenthetical citations with a quotation and a paraphrase.

Example 1. "Joe Califano, U.S. Secretary for Health in the 1980s, described smoking as 'slow-motion suicide'" (Haughton, 1996).

Example 2. Smokers lose an average of 12 to 15 years from their lives. Almost 50 percent of them die before retirement age (Haughton, 1996).

Discuss the following questions with your class.

1.   Which example is a paraphrase? ___ How do you know?
2.   Why does the paraphrase have an author-date citation?
3.   Is the author's first name or last name used in the citations?
4.   What is plagiarism?

C.   Read the sample research paper, "Slow-Motion Suicide," in this chapter and mark the passages that contain parenthetical citations. After you finish reading, answer the discussion questions and discuss your answers with the class.

Discussion Questions

1.   How long is this paper?

2.   How many quotations does the author use?

3. How many paraphrases does the author use?

4. What do these first three questions tell you about using paraphrases and quotes in a short research paper?

5. What kind of information makes up most of the paper?

6. What is the thesis statement for this paper?

7. Do the quotes and paraphrases cited provide important information that supports or proves the thesis?

8. What information is included in the citation? In what order?

9. Where are the citations placed in the sentence? Where is the punctuation placed?

Slow-Motion Suicide

Mindy Roth

WR 101

September 1, 1998

Smoking is glamorous, sophisticated, and cool. That is what the tobacco industry would like us to believe, but the truth is that smoking kills. Each year three million people die as a result of smoking. It is not instant death. "Joe Califano, U.S. Secretary for Health in the 1980s, described smoking as 'slow-motion suicide' " (Haughton, 1996). Smokers lose an average of 12 to 15 years from their lives. Almost 50 percent of them die before retirement age (Haughton, 1996).

Tobacco smoke contains thousands of chemicals, hundreds of which are poisonous and many known to cause cancer. Among the poisons are cyanide (used in gas chambers), arsenic, carbon monoxide (a gas in car fumes), ammonia, pesticide residues, and toxic metals. Many of these substances are not allowed to be dumped in garbage landfills yet smokers are inhaling them into their bodies. The most well-known poison in cigarettes is nicotine. Just 50 milligrams of pure nicotine on your tongue, the equivalent of one or two drops, would kill you immediately (Kowalski, 1997). Since the nicotine in cigarettes is not in its pure form, it doesn't kill smokers immediately.

The poisons in cigarette smoke cause damage to the human body. They injure or destroy lung tissue. They damage the cells lining the air passages and the air sacs in the lungs. This leads to chronic bronchitis and emphysema. Both of these lung diseases make even the simple act of breathing difficult, and both are a common cause of death among smokers. Smoking also causes cancer and is responsible for the majority of lung cancer deaths. Tobacco use also causes cancer of the mouth, throat, esophagus, kidney, pancreas, cervix, and bladder.

Nicotine, in combination with other substances found in cigarette smoke, is as addictive as heroin and cocaine. When taken in small amounts, nicotine produces pleasurable feelings to the smoker, feelings that make the smoker want to smoke more. It can make a person feel more alert, or it can have a calming effect. Later the body physically craves more and more nicotine in order to feel the effects. The smoker has become addicted. Smokers who want to stop smoking find it very difficult to quit. They suffer withdrawal symptoms such as irritability, drowsiness, mood swings, headaches, and depression.

So why do people who would normally stay as far away as possible from known cancer-causing substances choose to smoke? Most smokers have their first cigarette when they are adolescents. Many youths start because of peer pressure. Their friends use tobacco, so they try it too. They want to fit in, be cool, appear older. Statistics show that if a parent smokes, there is a greater chance that the children will smoke. Smoking is viewed as a sign of adulthood. Teens see film stars smoking in movies and wish to be like them. The tobacco companies spend billions of dollars a year on ads that show smoking as an exciting, sophisticated, fun, healthy adult activity.

Many teens believe they won't become addicted to cigarettes. Tobacco companies know they will. In a secret, in-depth study, a tobacco industry researcher in reference to young people who start smoking was quoted as saying, "The desire to quit and actually carrying it out are two quite different things, as the would-be quitter soon learns" (Pietrusza, 1997). According to the United Kingdom Health Education Authority, if teens continue to try smoking and people who already smoke don't quit smoking, it is estimated that by the year 2020, 10 million people a year will die worldwide as a result of tobacco use (Haughton, 1996). And it is not instant death; it is the result of long, painful diseases. It is slow-motion suicide.

References

Haughton, E. (1996). <u>A right to smoke?</u> New York: Franklin Watts.

Kowalski, K. M. (1997, February). Tobacco's toll on teens. <u>Current Health</u> <u>2</u>, 6–12.

Pietrusza, D. (1997). <u>Smoking</u>. San Diego: Lucent Books.

Work It Out: Part 1

Number the paragraphs in "Slow-Motion Suicide" and then analyze the organization of the paper by filling in the outline. You may choose to work alone, with a partner, or with the whole class. Change the structure of the outline as needed.

Outline

I. Introduction (__ number of paragraphs)
   A. The introduction grabs the reader's attention by

   B. Thesis statement (problem)

II. Paragraph #2
   A. Topic sentence (causes)

      1. Support
      •
      •
      •

III. Paragraph #3
   A. Topic sentence (effects/consequences)

      1. Support
      •
      •
      •

IV. Paragraph #4
    A. Topic sentence (effects/consequences)

        1. Support
        •
        •
        •

V. Paragraph #5
    A. Topic sentence (reasons)

        1. Support
        •
        •
        •

VI. Conclusion (outcomes)
    A. The author concludes the paper by

        1. Support
        •
        •
        •

Work It Out: Part 2

Answer the following questions.

1. Do all of the paragraphs support the thesis statement?
2. Think about the title of the article. Does the title arouse interest, introduce the topic, or indicate the direction the writing will take?
3. Does the article present more than one point of view?
4. Is the author neutral? How do you know?
5. What was the author's purpose in writing this paper?

Get Going

Research

1. **Choose three sources that contain important information about your topic and read them carefully.**

As you gather information you will find that many of the same facts and explanations are stated in each source. You will need to understand and remember what you read in order to use the information to support your thesis. Most of the information in your paper will be the facts and explanations that are common to many sources, but you must understand the information and explain the ideas in your own words, the way you do when you write a summary.

You will also want to paraphrase some passages and quote some sentences from your sources. These will be passages that are unique to one source and that support your thesis. Look back to Unit 7 for guidelines on choosing quotations and paraphrases.

2. **Identify passages you may want to quote or paraphrase as support in your research paper and copy them into a notebook. Choose passages that support your thesis. Avoid using too many paraphrases or quotations.**

3. **After reading your sources, reassess your preliminary thesis statement and make any changes you want to make to it.**

You have decided on your topic, gathered information and questions about it, and written a preliminary thesis statement that will help you to create a preliminary outline. One way to create a preliminary outline is to look back at the information you have gathered and sort the information that supports your thesis into categories or subtopics.

4. **Now look again at the information you have gathered. Sort it into categories or subtopics that work for your topic.**

After sorting information into categories or subtopics, you might find there are too many areas to cover in a short research paper, or during the research process, you may be unable to find enough information about a particular subtopic. If this happens, you might decide to drop a whole subtopic or parts of it.

5. **Use the information you have gathered and sorted to help you create a preliminary outline.**

This first outline is called preliminary because it may change as you make decisions about what information to include in your paper. Have your outline checked by your teacher.

Give-and-Take

This exercise will help you learn more about parenthetical citations and how to reference them. Work with a partner to fill in the blanks with the correct word. Choose from among the words given for each question-answer pair. When you have finished, compare your answers with the rest of the class.

1. Question: If you only include the author's _____ and the _____ of

publication in your parenthetical _____, how does the reader

know where you got your _____?

Answer: A list of the _____ you have _____ within the text of your

paper is found at the _____ of your paper on a page entitled

_____ or *Works Cited*.

citation	end	*References*
cited	information	sources
date	last name	

2. Question: What is the _____ for this list?

   Answer: This is an _____ list that follows the reference style chosen by

   your _____.

alphabetized
format
professor/instructor

3. Question: What _____ should you follow?

   Answer: In your paper, you are _____ the style manual _____

   Publication Manual of the American Psychological Association or a style

   sheet _____ by your teacher.

entitled	provided
following	style

Pull It Together: Part 1

So far in this unit,

- you have learned about the three-step approach to writing a research paper;
- you have brainstormed possible topics and limited your topic in a preliminary thesis statement;
- you have learned where to find sources and how to choose relevant passages to quote or paraphrase;
- you have learned what kind of information needs to be recorded about your sources;

- you have learned about using parenthetical citations within the text of your paper;
- you have read a sample research paper;
- you have read from at least three different sources about your own topic;
- you have categorized information into subtopics, which helped you to create a preliminary outline.

Now, review your thesis statement and outline and write the first draft of your paper. In your first draft, focus on bringing together all of the information you need to support or prove your thesis and to make your points clear. As you begin to write, consider your audience. What do they know about the topic? How might their background be different from yours? What will interest them? What questions might your readers have?

Pull It Together: Part 2

A. Three parts are included in the research paper "Slow-Motion Suicide": a title page, the text of the paper, and a reference page. Look at the title page. How is it formatted? Make a title page for your paper.

B. Include a reference page at the end of your paper. Look at the reference page at the end of the sample research paper "Slow-Motion Suicide" and follow the same format. Your teacher may provide you with a style sheet, or you can refer to the *Publication Manual of the American Psychological Association.*

Just Do It

Exchange your paper with a classmate. Read your classmate's paper and answer the following questions in your classmate's book.

1. What is the main idea of the paper?
2. Find the thesis statement and write it down.
3. Does each paragraph support or develop the main idea of the paper?
   __ yes   __ no

4. Does each paragraph have a topic sentence? Underline each topic sentence.

5. Do the supporting sentences contain enough details, examples, and concrete evidence to support the topic sentence?

    __ yes   __ no

    Paragraph(s) #_____ need(s) more details, examples, and concrete evidence to better support the topic sentence.

After you have finished answering the questions, give your answers and your classmate's paper back to your classmate. Make any changes you want to make to your own paper at this time.

Now give this draft to your teacher. Your teacher will use the following form, Fix It Up, to help you further revise your paper.

Fix It Up   Student's Name _____

1. The title arouses interest and tells the reader what the paper is about.

    __ yes   __ no

2. The introduction catches the reader's interest.

    __ yes   __ no

3. The thesis statement is clearly stated in the introduction.

    __ yes   __ no

4. The thesis statement adequately expresses the main idea.

    __ yes   __ no

5. Each paragraph supports or develops the main idea of the paper.

    __ yes   __ no

6. Each paragraph has a topic sentence.

    __ yes   __ no

7. The supporting points are clearly stated.

    __ yes   __ no

    __ They need to be explained more fully.

    __ They contain enough details, examples, and concrete evidence.

    __ Some should be eliminated.

    __ All of the examples are relevant.

8. The points are presented in a logical and useful order.

    __ yes   __ no

    You might want to move the following information.

9. The draft contains a strong conclusion that supports the paper.

    __ yes   __ no

Polish It

To prepare the final draft of your paper, read your teacher's comments in Fix It Up and make all of the necessary changes. Then edit your paper to correct any grammatical and/or mechanical problems. Use the checklist, Polish It, in the Appendix to help you polish your paper.

Evaluate Yourself   Name _____

Read the final draft of your paper and fill in the following form.

1. My title arouses interest and tells the reader what the paper is about.

    __ yes   __ no

2. My introduction catches the reader's interest.

    __ yes   __ no

3. My thesis statement is clearly stated in my introduction.

    __ yes   __ no

4. All of my ideas are related to the main point stated in my thesis statement.

    __ yes   __ no

5. Each paragraph has a topic sentence that clearly supports and develops the main idea of the paper.

    __ yes   __ no

6. I paraphrased material well. I expressed the unique ideas of the authors of my sources clearly and in my own words.

    __ yes   __ no

7. I supported my main points with enough details, examples, and concrete support.

    __ yes   __ no

8. I only included information that was necessary to explain or support my main points.

    __ yes   __ no

9. The conclusion of my paper supports the thesis statement.

    __ yes   __ no

10. I included a properly formatted reference page.

    __ yes   __ no

11. I included a properly formatted title page.

    __ yes   __ no

12. I edited my paper for spelling and word use, capitalization and punctuation, sentence structure, grammar, and format.

    __ yes   __ no

13. I'm having trouble with

Make any final changes you wish to make to your paper and give your paper, along with your self-evaluation, to your teacher.

Teacher Feedback

Student's Name _____

1. Your title arouses interest and tells the reader what the paper is about.
   __ yes __ no

2. Your introduction catches the reader's interest.
   __ yes __ no

3. Your thesis statement is clearly stated in your introduction.
   __ yes __ no

4. All of your ideas are related to the main point stated in your thesis statement.
   __ yes __ no

5. Each paragraph has a topic sentence that clearly supports and develops the main idea of the paper.
   __ yes __ no

6. You paraphrased material well. You expressed the unique ideas of the authors of your sources clearly and in your own words.
   __ yes __ no

7. You supported your main points with enough details, examples, and concrete support.
   __ yes __ no

8. You only included information that was necessary to explain or support your main points.
   __ yes __ no

9. Your conclusion supports your thesis.
   __ yes __ no

10. You included a properly formatted reference page.
    __ yes __ no

11. You included a properly formatted title page.
    __ yes __ no

12. Your paper was carefully edited for spelling and word use, capitalization and punctuation, sentence structure, grammar, and format.
    __ yes __ no

13. What I find most interesting about your paper is

14. Other comments

Live and Learn

Additional Activities and Journal Assignments

1. Many songs have been written to highlight world and social problems. Phil Collins's song "Another Day in Paradise" is about homelessness. Michael Jackson's song "Gone Too Soon" is about dying from AIDS. John McCutcheon sings "Step by Step, the Longest March" about unionizing. With your classmates, brainstorm titles of other songs that highlight a world problem. Listen to the songs. (You should first check with your institution to find out the established policies for using copyrighted material in the classroom.) Choose one song that particularly moves you and write a short research paper about the issue it raises. Remember to use the three-step approach of inquiring, investigating, and researching.

2. Find and analyze a short research paper on a topic other than smoking. What is the main idea of the paper? How is it organized? Which categories of information does the paper cover? What kind of support is presented, and how is it presented? What do you think about the title, introduction, and conclusion of the paper? Who was the intended audience? Did the author choose clear and interesting words to convey the ideas presented in the paper?

3. Look back at the paper "Slow-Motion Suicide." What title would you give this article? Would the title you give this paper depend on the audience for whom it was written? For instance, if the audience were all scientists would you give it a different title than if it were written for teenagers or for lawmakers? Who was the intended audience? How do you know? Brainstorm different audiences for the paper and titles to go with each audience.

4. Learn more about smoking and health by contacting Action on Smoking and Health, the American Cancer Society, the American Heart Association, the American Lung Association, Americans for Nonsmokers' Rights, or Youth Partnership for Health. Most of these organizations have websites on the Internet. In your journal, write a letter to a friend who smokes, sharing what you've learned about smoking.

5. Write a short research paper about a topic related to your major field of study, your current employment, or another interest you have. Remember to use the three-step approach of inquiring, investigating, and researching.

6. Look back at the papers you have written throughout this course and choose one to revise using the Fix It Up section in this unit and the Appendix, Polish It.

7. In your journal, describe what you have learned about writing while doing this unit.

8. Online Conferencing: The following activities in this unit provide good opportunities for online conferencing.

Get Set, Inquire: Part 1

1. Brainstorm topics online.
2. Choose one or two of the topics you came up with and brainstorm subtopics.

Get Set, Inquire: Part 2: Reply to your classmates' topics online.
Live and Learn #1: Brainstorm song titles online.
Live and Learn #3: Discuss alternatives for article titles online.

Appendix

Polish It

To prepare the final draft of your paper, you will need to edit your paper to correct any grammatical and/or mechanical problems. Use the following checklist to help you polish your paper.

Spelling and Word Use

__ 1. I have spell-checked my paper.
__ 2. I have chosen vocabulary that is appropriate to the topic.
__ 3. I have used a variety of words.

Capitalization and Punctuation

__ 1. I have put capital letters at the beginnings of all of my sentences.
__ 2. I have capitalized all proper names of people or places.
__ 3. I have used the correct punctuation for quotations.
__ 4. I have used appropriate punctuation after and within each of my sentences.
__ 5. I have used the correct punctuation for parenthetical citations. (Correct punctuation for parenthetical citations is covered in Unit 8.)

Sentence Structure

__ 1. I have checked all of my sentences and corrected any fragments and/or run-on sentences.
__ 2. I have checked my sentences for acceptable word order.
__ 3. I have varied my sentences in length and structure.

Grammar

__ 1. I have checked my paper for problems with subject-verb agreement.
__ 2. I have checked my paper for problems with word forms.
__ 3. I have checked my paper for problems with verb tense and form.
__ 4. I have checked my paper for problems with definite and indefinite articles.
__ 5. I have checked my paper for problems with prepositions.

Format (Format for a research paper is covered in Unit 8)

__ 1. I have included a title page.

__ 2. I have included the final edited version of my paper.

__ 3. I have included a properly formatted reference page.